Live at
John 10:10

Lisa J. Radcliff

LISA RADCLIFF

Hidden

With

Christ

Breaking Free from the Grip of Your Past

Hidden with Christ: Breaking Free from the Grip of Your Past

Copyright © 2018 Lisa J. Radcliff

ISBN-13: 978-1-54392-283-7 (paperback)
ISBN-13: 978-1-54392-284-4 (ebook)

Contents

Hidden Heroes

This is the book I never wanted to write. It is the story I never wanted told. It was supposed to stay hidden. Childhood sexual abuse is ugly, life changing, and very private. I wish this story had never happened. But it did. And it has a purpose. Perhaps one purpose is for someone like you to read it and find freedom from your past. That is my prayer in writing this book.

As I have gained perspective (translate "gotten old") on the abuse I endured, I can see that God placed certain individuals in my life to keep me from being completely swallowed up by the darkness swirling around me. I've labeled them heroes. They are the men that God used at precise times to help me in specific ways. Looking back now, I see how their influence provided a sense of safety. They also brought an understanding that not all men are bad, untrustworthy villains to be feared. Some, maybe even most, can be trusted and can be "God with skin on" when we need them to be.

If we're willing to look past the difficult memories, we can see God's hand in ways that we couldn't see at the time of our suffering. The "whys" may never be completely answered, but the "Where was God?" question can be. He was right there, in someone who helped, if only in a small way, to keep my feet from slipping or to pick me up after falling. Heroes were there, and we will see them if we look past our pain. They were evidence that I was always in the grip of God's grace.

I will introduce you to some of the heroes throughout my story. But there are many more who have entered my life over the years—pastors, husbands of friends, ministry partners, coworkers, and others—who are not mentioned but have been important to my healing.

The biggest hero is God himself. It was his Word that brought healing and freedom to my heart. It was there that I learned that my old life was dead, hidden with Christ in God (Colossians 3:3). He is completely trustworthy and only wants the very best for us. Unfortunately, some lessons need to be learned in dark places, but he is never far from us. We are never out of his sovereign care. And the darkness cannot overcome his light.

I have included several Bible passages that particularly helped me but are certainly not an exhaustive study of the topics. I encourage you to study God's Word for yourself. You will find answers, comfort, and freedom in the pages of Scripture. I have also included topics that have affected me or others I have talked to, but everyone is different and reacts differently to trauma. The general principles can apply to almost any problem area, so allow them to help you think through some of the difficult issues surrounding abuse. In an effort to inform parents and other caregivers about sexual abuse, I've included a section with some practical tips at the end of the book.

Since I am not a licensed counselor and have little training in counseling, what I share in this book should not be taken as professional advice. It is simply my experience and the experiences others have shared with me. A professional Christian counselor can help guide you along the journey that leads to freedom.

CHAPTER 1:

Losing My Grip

Villains and Heroes

"You misunderstood him. He's just overly friendly. He's like that with everyone."

Those words from my mother solidified my deepest fear: he was right. Other adults knew he was sexually abusing me, and they didn't care. He had been telling me that for close to a decade, since the first time at the community pool when he held me against him. Although I didn't understand what he was doing or what it was I was feeling pushing against me, I instinctively knew it wasn't right. Struggling to break free, I told him to let me go or I would tell my daddy, who was also standing in the water on the other side of the five-feet-deep section. He and my dad were just far enough away from each other to throw me back and forth, a game that had been a lot of fun for a little five-year-old girl—until that moment.

It was like a movie scene, when villain and hero meet but don't recognize each other. One was intent on getting what he wanted with no regard for my life, while the other wanted nothing more than my future happiness.

Hero Dad

My father was a gentle man. Ferdie, as we called him, never argued and never raised his voice. The strongest language he ever used was, "Oh, nuts," but things had to be pretty bad. Picture Dick Van Dyke once his hair turned white, and you'll have a visual of my dad. He had the same look and the same voice, and he was a klutz—always tripping over something. We shared July birthdays and always celebrated them together. I felt special, celebrating with him and sharing a certain kind of birthday cake only the two of us thought was the best in the world.

Of course, I don't remember our first meeting, but he wrote about it in a seminary English class:

> The early morning frost seemed to spread a heavenly appearance on the slightly changing landscape in the South-Eastern Pennsylvania countryside on this cool, crisp Wednesday morning as I sped north on the Turnpike. My destination was a town in Central Pennsylvania, where I had an appointment to meet, from what I had been told, a French girl.
>
> The trip, slowed by patches of early morning fog and yet cheerful because of the sunrise over the hills to my right, was a very happy journey. I spent much of my time thinking and wondering what she would be like. Would she be pretty? Would she be petite? What color hair and eyes would she have? Would she accept me? Many questions entered my heart, mind, and soul, and the excitement seemed to stream into the farthest reaches of every limb, causing tingling sensations, even to the tips of my

toes, seeming to force me to push on at an even greater speed than I normally would.

Arriving at the town where I was to meet her, I finally found the proper address, and at just the time that had been prearranged by all the letters and phone calls of the week before, I entered the building with trepidation and anxiety, so much that it seemed to tell me to sit down and compose myself. But my legs did not seem to be connected to my mind, and I pressed on at yet a faster pace. After finding the directory of the building, I just stood and studied it for a while to steady myself for an entrance. When I felt I had the physical ability to match my mental desires, I entered the elevator and arrived at the proper floor and room to meet my friend who was to greet me there. Soon he left the room and returned a short time later with Lisa.

There she was, the girl of my dreams. I went to her and took her in my arms and held her, but in a way that I could still see her every feature. Not a word was spoken as I looked into her large brown eyes, stroked her soft brown hair, and noticed the pink glow of warmth of her small ears, the cute little button nose flanked by plump rosy cheeks just waiting to be kissed, and the smile on her red lips.

She reached out and touched my eyes and my lips, and not being too sure of me, the smile seemed to disappear temporarily until after several minutes, she decided that I, too, was for her. The smile returned and a look of beckoning was apparent in the eyes which at first seemed a little sad, but now seemed to smile too. Still not a word was spoken, as I gave Lisa Jayne, my soon to be adopted daughter, to her new mother, whose eyes by this time were moist at the sight of this beautiful baby girl that the adoption agency had chosen for us after careful screening processes.

Now, along with Lori, another girl we had adopted a year earlier, we felt we were a complete family with the necessary love and means to grant the girls a new start in their young lives. Now all we can ask and pray for is much health and happiness as we all grow together.

Dad included a handwritten note to the professor that read, "This story is all true, except the ending, which I wish was."

My parents divorced when I was three years old and my sister was five. One of the things I admired about my dad was that he never spoke negatively about my mom. No matter what. Even if I was mad at my mom and ranting to him, he never jumped onto that bandwagon. As an adult, I realized that while Dad had a gentle spirit, he was very strong—the biblical term would be *meek*, a beautiful combination of strength and gentleness. He consistently chose to do the right thing, especially when it came to his girls.

Saturdays were Dad time. My sister and I were his every Saturday from ten a.m. till seven p.m. (sharp!). It was the highlight of my week. We would spend our Saturdays together canoeing a local canal, playing at the park, visiting the zoo, or just hanging out eating grilled cheese sandwiches. He taught me how to throw a football, how to fish, how to body surf in the waves at the Jersey Shore, and how to drive.

Dad loved to build things, especially his little N-gauge train platform. He once built a sailboat—a real, four-passenger sailboat. It was beautiful, with a glossy wood finish. We named it Willit, standing for "will it float?" And it did! He wasn't offended at all that we doubted its seaworthiness and proudly painted *WILLIT* in bright yellow letters on its shiny stern. I can't count how many times he flipped Willit while teaching himself how to sail it.

He could fix anything of mine that had broken, from mangled kites to my first car. When I say *fixed*, I really mean "McGyver'd." He made things so they would work again but not necessarily in the conventional way.

Dad couldn't cook, so sometimes we ate cold hot dogs for lunch and TV dinners for supper. Fortunately, when I was nine years old, he married my stepmother, who is an excellent cook. And once he retired, he learned to bake cookies.

Going places with Dad was always an adventure because he never went the same way twice. He had lots of different cars as I was growing up. One was an adorable Volkswagen Bug convertible. He would let me shift gears while he drove, nodding when it was time for me to shift. Not one to panic, he waited patiently for me to find the right gear, only lending a hand if the Bug had slowed too much to shift into a higher gear. A few years later, he bought a baby blue 1964 Impala. It was an enormous car. He would take me to an empty parking lot, sit me on his lap, and let me steer the behemoth around the lot (occasionally bumping curbs). Dad was the most patient man I have ever known.

It was Dad who got my sister and me our first dog, a two-year-old scraggly mutt named Fifi, from the SPCA. That was one of the happiest days of my childhood. When I first saw her, she was poking her little gray nose through the kennel enclosure. I bent down to touch it, and she wagged her tail. I was instantly in love.

With Lori and I begging to take Fifi home, he said, "We have to call your mom first." She would have to give her okay before we could adopt her. Those were the longest few minutes of my life. I was sure she would say no, but she didn't. I imagine they had this planned ahead of time or things wouldn't have gone so smoothly.

Dad's real joy was singing. He loved music and was quite talented. In his younger days, he was first drummer in the famous Philadelphia drum and bugle corps Reilly Raiders. More than anything else, Dad loved to sing Barbershop harmony. He was a charter member of the local Barbershop chorus. He sang baritone in several quartets, arranged or composed music for them, and served as director of the chorus for a short time. Shortly after his death, he was inducted into the Barbershop Harmony Society's Hall of Fame.

I loved to sing too. My junior choir practice took place on Saturday mornings at nine a.m., so Dad would pick me up at the church for our Saturday time together. Often, he would arrive early so he could come in and listen to our practice. Our director would occasionally ask his advice, which would make me to beam with pride.

My very favorite times were spent curled next to him, watching a football game, eating peanuts, and tracing the lines of the impressive football-related scar on his arm. He had been a football player, a navy sailor, and a firefighter, and next to him I felt safe and loved. Whether we were at the zoo or an amusement park, or working on a project, Saturdays with Dad were the best days of my youth. I hated the last hour or so of Saturday nights with him. It was hard to take my eyes off the clock as the minutes with him ticked down. But I knew he was never far away and that I could go to him anytime I needed to—and I needed to a lot.

Everyone's Friend

Swimming was another favorite activity for Dad and me. We were both at home in the water, either jumping waves in the ocean or swimming the width of the pool underwater. Since I was only with him on Saturdays, I cherished the time we spent together at the pool. In my childish way of thinking, it didn't occur to me that he couldn't see what was going on under the water, especially without his glasses. So when Mr. R said that my dad knew what was happening and he didn't care, I believed him.

Mr. R was a popular man in our town. He was well known and well liked by both adults and children. Friendly and charismatic, he had a way of making others believe that he cared about them. Due to his position with the post office, he knew everyone in town and everyone knew him. Then when he retired from the post office, he took a job as a school bus driver.

Parents trusted him with their little ones; he would welcome them onto his bus with the aura of a loving grandpa. He even earned our local newspaper's "Bus Driver of the Month" award because of his friendliness. The local newspaper printed the story on the front page, along with a picture of him next to his bus. The article described how he had pet names for all the little girls on his bus. The warning signs that he might be a pedophile were obvious and ignored. "It's just his way," people would say. Surely this pillar of the community, deacon in his church, and everyone's friend couldn't be a danger to children.

Most of my encounters with Mr. R occurred during the summer at the community pool over several years. Mr. R's house sat directly between my house and the pool, and sometimes he would stop me when I was walking to or from the pool. It confused me. He was my dad's friend, and I thought he was my friend.

He wasn't someone I dreaded seeing or tried to steer clear of. Sometimes he was just plain nice. Not many adults in my life seemed at all interested in me or talked to me. But he did. Sometimes we would sit on the grassy bank at the back of his property, which faced the road to the pool, and just talk. He seemed genuinely interested in what I thought and what I had to say. He would wave to people driving by and would receive friendly waves or honks in return. At other times, he would be working in his garden, and I would stop to chat with him and he would give me fresh produce to take home for my mom.

Plenty of my encounters with him included no abuse whatsoever. I liked him, and liked being with him. But on some occasions, the way he touched me made me uncomfortable. I was young and naïve. Not having a dad or brother at home, I had no knowledge of male anatomy, let alone how men think or act. The times that he held me close to him or sat me on his lap were uncomfortable and confusing.

When he touched me, I became even more confused. What did I feel? Was I afraid of him? Did I love him? What was this all about? His reaction to it made me think it must be a good thing. Was this what love felt like? As I write this, close to forty years later, I can still smell his cologne and hear his moaning. But it doesn't have the hold over me that it once did. We'll talk about the freedom I found (and that can be yours) later on.

CHAPTER 2:

In the Grip of Suspicion

Hero Knight

The start of my fifth-grade year of school brought a major change. Our school had a new fifth-grade teacher, Mr. Knight. On the first day of school, all the kids, in their best "first day of school" outfits, were gathered in the gym/cafeteria to be assigned to their classes and teachers.

The school had two fifth-grade classes, and when I heard my name called to get into Mr. Knight's line, fear set in and then morphed into a flight response. Ignoring instructions, I snuck into the other teacher's line instead. Miss Haradin, an old maid who lived with her twin sister a few blocks from the school, made every fifth grader shake in their boots. We all suspected she was a witch—a real one. But I decided the witch teacher was a better option than the man teacher. It didn't take long for them to figure out I was in the wrong line and correct the problem.

Mr. Knight was young for an adult. Fresh out of college, he was in his very first teaching position. He seemed excited about it. I wished he had been hired somewhere else. But I soon learned there was something different about him: he was fun. He did a lot of hands-on teaching, including a science lesson that took us to the local creek to catch crayfish. At recess, instead of huddling with the other teachers, Mr. Knight was the pitcher for kickball.

He didn't get upset if his students fooled around a little during class, and he had an easy smile but stayed in command of his classroom. We all knew how far we could go with our antics and when it was time to buckle down and do the work. I don't remember Mr. Knight ever raising his voice. He didn't need to.

But he did discipline his students. If you did something deserving of punishment, he would have you sit with your back against the wall, like you were sitting in a chair, but without the chair. You had to hold that position for one minute. I never did anything to warrant this reprimand, but I tried it at home to see what it felt like. One minute in that position was painful! I resolved to never have to do that in class.

In some ways, he was quite different from the other teachers in our school. He never wore a suit. While teaching, he sat on the back of a wooden desk chair with his feet on the seat. He would roll the chalk between his hands as he talked, and it clicked as it rolled over his wedding ring. I remember thinking it was a cool sound, and I was pretty sure he rolled the chalk just to hear that sound. He would get excited when one of his students figured out a problem or answered a question, and his enthusiasm for learning was genuine and contagious.

His classroom door was outfitted with a chin-up bar. If we wanted to, we could do a chin-up going in or out of class. We even held competitions to see who could do the most chin-ups. It always came down to the same two kids, Billy and Cindy. I never tried. I knew I could manage one chin-up but was too shy to do it in front of the other kids. Mr. Knight would cheer on each kid's effort as if an Olympic medal were at stake.

The only thing I didn't like about him was that if you needed help doing work at your desk, he would lean over you from behind. At first, this freaked me out, but nothing bad ever happened. Eventually, rather than being frozen in fear, I found a sense of safety in it. I believed I could trust him.

Toward the end of the school year, I needed a cast on my leg from hip to ankle. Mr. Knight became protective of me, making sure I was comfortable in class and not overdoing it at recess. I was already klutzy, so being unable to bend one leg only made things worse. Mr. Knight gave me the nickname *Boom-Boom* because I was always running into things, and the cast made a loud boom as it crashed into chairs and desks. He changed my opinion of men. I will never forget the difference he made in my life.

Over the years, I would stop in to see him, and he was always happy to chat for a while. Thirty years later, I got in touch with him. He wasn't difficult to find since he was still teaching fifth grade at the same school, although he planned to retire the following year. He invited me to speak to his class about my work with Seeing Eye® dogs, and I was thrilled for the opportunity.

The day arrived for my visit. He greeted me with a huge smile and hug. His wife and granddaughter were there too. We went into the same gym/cafeteria where I had eaten thousands of income-based free lunches and passed the Presidential Physical Fitness test, my number-one accomplishment of elementary school. It was exactly the same—skinny pine floors with a high gloss finish and cafeteria tables folded up along the walls, only it seemed smaller.

As I took my place in front of the students and my former teacher, butterflies filled my stomach, just like when we had to stand and recite the multiplication table in his class. He gave me an A for my talk and another hug as we said goodbye.

It wasn't until that day that I realized how much of an impact he had on my life. I looked at his current crop of fifth graders and wondered how many other kids he had positively influenced, if not saved, in thirty years of teaching. God had placed this special teacher in my life at the time I needed him most.

Trust

Trust does not come easily for abused children. Their world is turned upside down. People they thought were trustworthy betrayed them. It breaks my heart that some kids can't even trust their own dads or other adults closest to them.

But they don't have to lose trust in all adults. Sunday School teachers, school teachers, coaches, pastors, and parents of friends can play an important role in a child developing or regaining trust. I was very blessed to have a loving dad and a protective teacher in my life as a young child. Because of them, my ability to trust people was not completely destroyed. In time, trusting them became easy because of how they treated me. Trust was cultivated through my relationships with them because they never gave me reason *not* to trust them.

Other people in my life broke my trust and made it difficult for me to trust others. It had to be earned, and once broken, I found it impossible to trust that person again. To this day it is hard for me to trust people. I am always skeptical of others' motives, something

I need to constantly work on. Trust is built when promises are kept, and when someone sticks with you no matter what.

No one is more trustworthy than Jesus. He loved you so much, he died for you, but his love didn't end there. He prays for you. He cares for you. You can trust him with every part of your life, and he won't let you down. He keeps his promises, and his Word tells us that those promises are magnificent. One of my favorite promises is "I give them eternal life, and they will never perish, and no one will snatch them out of my hand. My Father, who has given them to me, is greater than all, and no one is able to snatch them out of the Father's hand" (John 10:28–29). Trusting that he's got me, and that he won't let go, brings peace—the peace that passes all understanding, regardless of the circumstances.

Stephen Curtis Chapman's songs on his album *Beauty Will Rise* are incredibly honest and moving. He wrote them following the tragic death of his youngest daughter. I have found great comfort in the words and principles he expresses and recommend anyone who is hurting get the CD. Each song exudes profound grief but always ends in trusting God. The honesty of not wanting his current circumstances to be his reality, for it to go away, to wake up from the nightmare, is stark and welcome.

Sometimes those in the Christian community keep smiling and hide their pain in the face of tragedy. They wrongly feel that if they show their heartbreak, they're somehow less Christian than those who stoically plod along. God can handle our sorrow, even if it comes with questioning his plan or anger at the circumstances.

You probably know that feeling of being in so much emotional pain that you can't bear to even think another thought. It's just too painful. At times like that, if you know God, then you know you can trust him. You start by telling yourself what you know about him, like "he is good," "his love is strong," and "his plans for me are better than my own."

Satan would love for you to doubt God during difficult times. But be like the tree in Psalm 1 that is planted by streams of water, whose leaf does not wither and whose roots go down deep. Learn who God is through his Word so that when the storms of life blow, you are firmly planted in him—the one who is completely trustworthy. It is a decision to trust God, not a feeling. Don't rely on feelings during the storms of life.

Trusting others is about giving up control. It's hard for us to give up control, especially with a history of abuse. Abusers control us through manipulation. They make us believe lies. They keep us silent, and they convince us that they are the only ones we can trust. But God says to "commit our way to the LORD; trust in him, and he will act" (Psalm 37:5). That means trusting God for every step forward. He's there to catch us when we fall, but even more, he wants us to trust him before taking that first step and watch what he will do. He promises to act, guiding our steps and shining light in dark places as we trust him.

Why is he trustworthy? Because he is Truth. Jesus proclaimed that he is the way, the truth, and the life (John 14:6). He is not just any truth, but *the* truth. The *I Am*'s of Jesus are especially comforting to those who have suffered abuse. Just think what it would mean to a child (or an adult who was abused as a child) to learn that Jesus is the door (John 10:7). He keeps out the bad guys, and his sheep can rest in safety. These are truths and word pictures that children can grasp and hold onto and ultimately find peace in. Psalm 86:11 says, "Teach me your way, O LORD, that I may walk in your truth." We don't have to ever wonder if God is telling us the truth. He cannot lie. His Word is true, so it is trustworthy.

Trust God with your life—your plans, your dreams, and your desires. Trust God even when the plans he has for you might not look like you would think (or hope). Proverbs 3:5 tells us, "Trust in the LORD with all your heart and lean not on your own understanding." You can trust that his plan is best and will be a blessing to you. Childhood sexual abuse seems like something that couldn't possibly be part of God's plan, but he can use it in ways you would never dream. It was through times of deepest trial that I learned to lean on God and trust him more fully. And out of that trust came great blessing. Cling to God when you can't understand where he's leading.

My favorite Bible story is found in the book of Daniel, when Daniel's friends were about to be thrown into the fiery furnace for refusing to bow down to the king's image. Their response to the king was, "Our God whom we serve is able to deliver us from the furnace of blazing fire; and he will deliver us out of your hand, O king. But even if he does not, let it be known to you, O king, that we are not going to serve your gods or worship the image that you have set up" (Daniel 3:17–18).

They didn't know which way things would go for them, but they trusted God and remained obedient to him. I'm sure they never expected to be walking around in the furnace with him and to walk out of it without even the scent of smoke on them. But that's what happened. Imagine what this experience did for their trust in God.

Do you trust God with *all* your heart for *all* areas of your life? Is there anything you are withholding, thinking you can't trust God with it? Commit those things to him in prayer. Ask him for the faith to trust him fully.

CHAPTER 3:

In the Grip of Fear

No One's Friend

Summer of that year ushered into my life the scariest person I would know: my stepmother's first husband, Bob. I had never met him, but what I knew about him was frightening. He was an angry, abusive man who drank too much.

Bob had a rough start to life. The son of an unwed mother in the late 1920s, he was unwanted and considered a disgrace. After his birth, he lived with an aunt and uncle who despised having him, which led to years of abuse. My stepmother recounted, "When Bob was a young boy, he came home excited about something he had done at school. He wanted to show his aunt and uncle and was running around the house calling for them. The noise made his uncle furious, and he screamed at Bob to shut up and knocked him down the stairs. His back was broken, but Bob's guardians refused to get him medical care. From that time on, Bob had a hunch in his back." It's not difficult to understand where Bob's anger and evil nature began.

While he did not sexually abuse me, Bob certainly was abusive in other ways and the source of most of the fear that ruled my early years. Bob and my stepmother lived in Maine, where he was a parole officer and she was a teacher. They were married for twenty-five turbulent years. He had abandoned her and been living in California for two years when she sought a divorce. It was then that he came back, angrier than ever.

Bob came to the house to pick up some of his things. He was grumbling while taking apart a piece of furniture. Finally, his anger exploded, and he wheeled around with a screwdriver in his hand. He backed my stepmother up against the kitchen sink with the screwdriver to her neck. She prayed for help, thinking this was it, he was going to kill her. God answered her prayer. Bob backed off and left the house.

When my dad heard the story (he was the pastoral intern at her church—long story), he told her the only way she would be safe was if she left the area. He proposed marriage. Within days, she moved to Pennsylvania to start a new life.

One of the best things about my stepmother was that she came with a little red log cabin in the backwoods of Maine. It was tiny, like a rustic dollhouse—only one room that housed a kitchen along the back wall and two single beds in the front, separated by a table and chairs positioned in front of a large window that looked out over the beautiful lake. A central fireplace and a ladder to the sleeping loft completed the floor plan. My dad took us there for a visit, and I instantly fell in love. The aroma of the fir trees took my breath away. The cabin was a place of complete peace and serenity, twenty miles from the nearest town.

The cabin, or *camp* as it's called in Maine, didn't have electricity or indoor plumbing. As a nine-year-old, I thought it was great; even using an outhouse was fun. I noticed some holes in the door, and that was my first introduction to Bob's personality. My stepmother told us, "Bob was here with some hunting buddies. One of them was using the outhouse, but Bob thought he was taking too long, so he started using his shotgun to hurry him along." The toilet seat is right inside the door, so this method of hurrying a visitor worked!

My dad and stepmother married in September 1973. From the start, Bob tormented them with phone calls and empty threats. He would call to say he had done something to the camp. Our caretakers would drive out to it and report back that everything was fine. But one night, Bob's threats became reality. He burned it down.

First, he took one of his prize possessions, a five-feet-wide floor-to-ceiling curtain made of beer tabs, and threw it in the lake. After dousing the camp with kerosene, Bob then stood in the middle and struck a match. The camp and everything in it was reduced to ashes. Everything but Bob.

When my dad and stepmother came to my mom's house that night to tell us what had happened, I was scared. I pictured that little red log cabin on fire, the furniture and decorations, even the beautiful birch bark canoe engulfed in flames. But what would come next was even more scary.

Although badly burned, Bob escaped the flames and drove to our caretaker's house, five miles away. With third-degree burns over 90 percent of his body, he was rushed to the hospital. There he was stabilized and eventually moved to a rehab in Canada, where he would recover over the next year. He was charged with and convicted of arson but never served any jail time. The authorities determined he had suffered enough, plus as a parole officer, he was part of "the system."

Bob returned to Maine with no eyelids, no ear, no nose, and plenty of scars. We heard from people who saw him that he was so disfigured, it was difficult to look at him. The only things about him that remained unchanged were his anger and violent nature. Everyone, including the local sheriff, was afraid of him. He had been scary before, but now he was described as a monster straight out of a Stephen King novel (SK lived less than an hour away, by the way).

The following summer, while we were vacationing at the newly built camp, Bob showed up. Our new camp was bigger than the little red log cabin but still a camp—a bare bones lakeside seasonal cabin with no electricity, no phone, and no indoor plumbing, but plenty of wildlife, canoeing, swimming, stargazing, reading by lamp light, and making s'mores in the fireplace.

Normally, camp was the most peaceful place on earth, far away from civilization and all its noise. But Bob's return destroyed the tranquility. Our once-carefree canoe rides turned into tense expeditions as we nervously scanned the shoreline for any sign of Bob among the rocks and trees. We were like bigfoot hunters, always peering into the woods and seeing unidentifiable shapes duck away, but never a confirmed sighting.

The mournful call of the loons after dark, once a soothing sound, took on an eerie cry that caused the hair on our necks to stand on end. Going to the outhouse in the dark was out of the question—it could wait until morning. Darkness in rural Maine is as black as tar and feels as thick. Lying in bed at night, I couldn't tell if my eyes were open or shut. But now that darkness was cloaked in something even darker.

During our time there, Bob parked his Jeep in the Y in the road—the only way in and out—a few hundred yards from our camp. With a shotgun across his lap, he made everyone on the lake uneasy. Just sitting there. Waiting. He was there every day. I was terrified of him.

More than once, Dad scooped us into the car and bounced down the dirt roads faster than usual. Using the phone at the lake house several miles away, we would call the sheriff, fearing Bob was about to get violent. The sheriff always promised to come out but never showed up. Not once.

At one point, Bob broke into the abandoned camp next to ours, only feet away. We heard glass shattering and then the loud creak of the rusty spring on the screen door. He was right next door. He could see us. Every time we looked out the window or stepped outside, we expected to see a horrifying creature with no nose and a drippy ear. (That was how people described him after the fire. They had been walking down the camp road as Bob fled for help, with his body still smoldering and the effects of the heat and flames grotesquely apparent.) Now he was close enough to hear our conversation, monitor our activity, maybe even feel our fear. Why wouldn't someone help us?

Dad slept with a loaded rifle under the bed. My fear level went through the roof. I feared seeing Bob's disfigured face, feared what he would do, feared being chased through the dense woods, and feared being killed. I had nightmares of stumbling into the woods, tripping over rocks, and getting slapped and scraped by branches, with Bob chasing after me. The Maine woods are so dense that venturing in only twenty feet can get you disoriented. Bob knew the woods and I didn't.

In my dreams, he either caught me or I was lost in the woods forever. This also solidified my fear of men, not to mention my fear of the dark, confined spaces, and bats (or any other creepy creatures).

Years later, my stepmother confided, "I never thought he would really kill us, except that one time." I'm glad she hadn't mentioned that at the time.

Fortunately, by the end of the summer, some of our neighbors reached their breaking point with Bob's intimidation. Since the sheriff wouldn't do anything about it, they took matters into their own hands. I don't know exactly what happened. Well after dark one night, there was a knock at the door. At once, our heads all snapped in the direction of the front door. Was it him?

Dad looked out the window, said, "It's okay," and then went to the door. In the darkness, I couldn't see much, but I could make out men with guns and dogs. I recognized one of them as a neighbor and friend from up the road. They spoke with my dad and my stepmother outside while my sister and I peeked out the window, straining to see and hear what was going on.

After several minutes, they left, and after that, Bob disappeared. Of course, there was always the fear that he would come back.

Fear

As Christians, we are admonished not to be fearful, that God has not given us a spirit of fear but of power and love and self-control (2 Timothy 1:7). But abuse can cause us to become fearful. Fear manifests itself in many ways—fear of people, particularly men or women, depending on the gender of our abuser, or of a myriad of other fears. We know the Bible rhetorically says, "The Lord is my helper; I will not fear; what can man do to me?" (Hebrews 13:6). That sounds good, but unfortunately we have experienced what man can do to us, and that is exactly what we are afraid of.

So how can we overcome our fear?

As a child, I was afraid of nearly everything, but most afraid of men. After reading about Bob, you can probably understand why. Fear monopolized my life. It kept me from doing things or trying new things. And although I can now say with confidence that there aren't many people I fear, not all my fears have been conquered.

I am extremely claustrophobic. And it's weird claustrophobia. Elevators don't bother me but cities do. I mean, how can you not see those skyscrapers swaying and moving closer together? It's so obvious. Anytime I feel closed in without a way of escape, I tend to get very anxious.

One Sunday morning (okay, more than one) at the close of the worship service, both ends of my pew were blocked by people chatting in the aisles. I almost became an Olympic hurdler to get out. And don't ever tuck in my bed sheets. My foot must be able to escape the sheets at all times.

I also have a completely irrational fear of bridges. Doing deep breathing exercises seems to help while crossing them. I think the thought of my car plunging off a bridge reminds me of the deep darkness that almost consumed me during the time of my abuse. Or I'm just terrified at the thought of my car plunging off a bridge. And then there are bees, bats, and tractor-trailers.

Knowing my fears are irrational does not keep them from feeling real. Panic sets in, my heart races, my hands sweat—it's for real. But I also know that it's not real. Usually I can talk myself out of reacting to it and keep from embarrassing those with me. Sometimes I just have to get out of the situation. And sometimes that's best, although hurdling a pew would only end in embarrassment. Quietly exiting a situation is preferred.

My family has "helped" me deal with my fears by exploiting them. This has actually made them seem a lot less scary. For instance, if I'm standing on a chair screaming about a mouse in the house, my sons will toy with it. When my dog catches a snake, my husband tells him to take it to Mommy. My precious baby boy sent me a Facebook video taken from a car dash camera, showing a plane crashing into the bridge the car is crossing. (I didn't mention the fear of a plane landing on my car—it could happen). He thought it was great because it had a bunch of my fears all in one short video. That's cool. I send him shark videos all the time. Payback.

An important part of having good emotional health is not taking yourself too seriously. Yes, we have experienced serious things, but never lose your sense of humor. Being able to laugh at yourself and the "weird" things about yourself is very freeing.

Someday I may seek professional help for my fears, rather than trust in my less-than-sympathetic family to help me through. The truth is my fears really don't bother me all that much. They don't keep me from doing anything or interfere with my normal routine. And they entertain my family.

Even so, fear can be crippling. If that's the kind of fear you're dealing with, find a counselor and work toward freedom from it. Romans 8:15 tells us, "For you did not receive the spirit of slavery to fall back into fear, but you have received the Spirit of adoption as sons, by whom we cry, 'Abba, Father!'"

Do your fears enslave you, keeping you from the joy your life should have? As an adopted child of God, you should not allow yourself to be a slave to anything. He has set you free. One of the things I really like about this verse is that it makes God so personal.

I get the impression that we can yell, "Dad!" when we are afraid, and God comes running to our aid.

There are more reasons for a lot of my fears, which are not a part of this book (you'll have to read the next one). But whatever the reason, acknowledge your fears and ask God to give you courage. He tells us to be strong and courageous. Abuse victims who have survived and are seeking freedom from the past *are* strong and courageous!

Trust God and get his Word into your heart to help you on the journey. God's Word is full of stories of courage. As you study it, the Holy Spirit will apply it to your heart, and you will feel your heart changing from fearful to courageous. And remember, even in the worst situation possible, God is your help and you do not need to fear.

Do you know that whenever God says, "Do not be afraid" in His word, a promise follows? Here are some examples:

- "Do not be afraid to go down to Egypt, for there I will make you a great nation" (Genesis 46:3).

- "Do not be afraid … with me you shall be in safekeeping" (1 Samuel 22:23).

- "Do not be afraid … my God will not leave you nor forsake you" (1 Chronicles 28:20).

- "Do not be afraid … for the battle is not yours, but God's" (2 Chronicles 20:15).

- "You will not be afraid; when you lie down, your sleep will be sweet" (Proverbs 3:24).

- "Do not be afraid, for I am with you to deliver you" (Jeremiah 1:8).

- "Do not be afraid … your wife Elizabeth will bear a son" (Luke 1:13).

- "Do not be afraid; from now on you will be catching men" (Luke 5:10).

- "Do not be afraid, but go on speaking and do not be silent, for I am with you and no one will attack you to harm you" (Acts 18:9–10).

These are just a sampling of God's promises. Be strong and courageous; there is nothing to fear in the safety God offers his children. Deuteronomy 33:12 assures us, "The beloved of the Lord dwells in safety. The High God surrounds him all day long."

CHAPTER 4:

In the Grip of Sin

Giving Up/Giving In

During my junior high years, I had an unusual respite from the abuse. Although most people would call it a time of suffering, it really was a time to heal and be removed from some of the ugliness in my life.

I became very sick with the flu; it just wouldn't go away. I missed a lot of school through November and December, and as I started to feel better, my upper back started hurting. Tests showed that the flu virus had settled into the discs in my spine, eating them away. The cure was four months in a body cast.

I entered the hospital to have it done and spend a few days letting it dry. First, they fitted a neck brace that would hold my head in place. It started at my chin and ended on my chest. Then they plastered over it, covering my body in casting from my neck to my hips. I could sit up and walk around. Lying down was difficult, so I had to stay in a semi-sitting position. Washing my hair was an act worthy of Ringling Bros.

Because I wasn't supposed to move around much, I received homebound instruction. Instead of going to school, school came to me. I loved it. I could stay in my house, doctor's orders. No dealing with the outside world. No encounters with Mr. R. I could make myself grilled cheese sandwiches every day and watch soap operas. Life was good. I now believe I needed that respite before the next phase of my life started.

High school brought changes in schools, friends, experiences, and my own body. I had gone from awkward junior higher to shapely high schooler. Mr. R was very interested in my blossoming figure, and he let me know.

The summer between ninth and tenth grade was the worst. It was during that time that I had the infamous conversation with my mom described in chapter one. I don't know why I didn't try telling my dad or my stepmother. If my mom didn't believe me, I didn't think anyone else would. Mr. R was my dad's friend, so I thought my dad would be even less likely to believe he was a pedophile. After that conversation, I gave up and gave in. Mr. R was giving me attention that I now craved. He had awakened in me new feelings and passions that were not meant to be awakened yet. When my body responded to his touch, I didn't understand what was happening. He took advantage of my confusion, and the abuse escalated.

Where Are the Heroes?

The consequences of abuse can be expressed through different reactions from one victim to another. One person may react with a heightened sexual desire, interest in pornography, masturbation, or other forms of sexual expression. Still another may have a lack of sexual desire in marriage, the inability to have close relationships, or feelings of same-sex attraction. Many won't or can't see a professional counselor, and the church has historically turned away from talking about these kinds of issues. The shame caused by their response keeps victims from confiding in a Christian friend or ministry leader. As well, telling them that what they're feeling is wrong and giving them some Bible verses to prove it, will only solidify their shame and cause them to remain silent and never find freedom from their past.

It's natural to want to hide our sin. The first time I talked to someone about masturbation, they were shocked—shocked that I brought it up and shocked that it is a sin. They reasoned that it was the abuser who got them aroused and they had to masturbate to end the arousal. Another person said, "Once you've been sexually active and then you aren't, you have to satisfy your urges somehow. Masturbation is the private, harmless way to do that." No, it is sin. Anything outside of marriage that involves sexual fulfillment is sin. And you need to control it or it will control you.

While the abuse is not your fault, if you participated in sin because of it, you need to seek forgiveness. Victims don't get a pass because someone else's sin drove them to sin. They need to take responsibility for anything they have done that is contrary to God's Word. Many of the things mentioned above—pornography, addiction, abusing your body—are sin and need to be confessed and abandoned.

Held Captive by Sin

Often, victims who don't know what to do with their feelings become addicted to alcohol, drugs, food, or some other substance to numb the pain and erase the memories. I have spoken to many women who turned to food for comfort because they had no one to confide in.

While I was talking with one woman who was contemplating bariatric surgery, she revealed, "I used food for comfort, but then as I gained weight, I thought maybe if I became obese, I wouldn't be desirable to men." We talked about the underlying reason for her obesity and the need to repair that. Without freedom from her past, the benefits of surgery wouldn't last, heaping on more shame.

These issues are serious and can be extremely difficult to overcome. For some people, an addiction disappears at the moment of their salvation, but more often, it takes time and a mountain of effort to conquer addictive behaviors. Let's face it, addictions are something we do over and over and over. It shouldn't surprise us when we think we are over it but then fall back into it again. That's the nature of addiction. Thank God that he is merciful and slow to anger!

The apostle Paul laments, "For I do not understand my own actions. For I do not do what I want, but I do the very thing I hate" (Romans 7:15). Those of us who have struggled to overcome sin say a hearty "Amen!" to that. We totally get it. We're relieved to learn that even an apostle understands the struggle.

Too often, we assume something is wrong with us if we struggle with a particular sin. But, really, it's when we aren't struggling against sin that we should worry. When we know have a weakness, we will be on guard. But when we believe we can't possibly sin, we're in trouble. Sin is deceitful, and Satan loves to trip us up by making us feel secure in ourselves.

We have so many things to help us in our journey to freedom. One of those is God's Word, which is full of encouragement and instruction, not to mention love and mercy.

As part of the journey to freedom from sin and the past, I suggest memorizing these verses from Romans 6: "Let not sin therefore reign in your mortal body, to make you obey its passions. Do not present your members to sin as instruments for unrighteousness, but present yourselves to God as those who have been brought from death to life, and your members to God as instruments for righteousness. For sin will have no dominion over you, since you are not under law but under grace" (vv. 12-14). As Christians, we have been set free from the power of sin. Sin only has the power that we allow it to have.

You may be thinking, *Wait a minute. You just said that it's wrong to just give a victim Bible verses and send them on their way.* And you're right. But Scripture is the only thing that can truly change a heart. As an author, I can't sit down and listen to every reader's story. It's not possible for me put an arm around you and offer comfort other than the words of this book. But I know that God's Word is living and active and can give the peace that victims so desperately desire. I urge you to find Christians who will come alongside you to help navigate the road to freedom.

That one trusted friend can be crucial because they can give you accountability. Find that person who is willing to check in with you and challenge your decisions. Sometimes just knowing that someone is going to ask about how you're doing in a sinful area of your life is just what you need to get you past that sin.

More than Conquerors

I refer to Romans 8 often throughout this book. It's a good chapter to hunker down in. Verse 37 tells us, "No, in all this we are more than conquerors through him who loved us." Here we find that we can overwhelmingly conquer sin. Jesus is interceding for us, and we are living in his power, in the power of his resurrection.

Because Jesus has already conquered sin and death, we can too. He has opened the door to be able to conquer sin, even habitual sin that seems to have such a grip that you think you could never be free. When the first thought of that sin enters your mind, stop it right there. Don't dwell on it. Don't give Satan any opportunity at all. Acknowledge that it is sin and that you choose not to continue in it. Then ask God for help through his power, the power that has already conquered sin.

If the thought still isn't leaving you, call that friend and tell them your struggle. Pray with them. There is power in prayer, especially when joined with another believer. We are encouraged to bear one another's burdens and confess our sins to one another. It's part of being in the family of God. We can draw on the strength of one another. And don't forget that Jesus sent a Helper, the Holy Spirit, who lives within us and is able to keep us from falling. Call on him for help.

Are you a survivor or a conqueror? Just barely holding on, or overcoming and ruling? For me, it's not enough to just survive. As a teenager, I had a poster in my room with a picture of a kitten hanging from the end of a rope by its claws with the phrase *Hang on, baby, Friday's coming!* That's not me. I more than survived; I conquered my past and the sin associated with it. I didn't just survive, I thrived.

I want you to completely conquer the things that keep you from the abundant life Jesus offers you. If you are trusting in yourself to get over your past, you will just be a survivor. When you trust in God's power to heal, you will be a conqueror.

CHAPTER 5:

In the Grip of Darkness

One hot summer day as I walked home from the pool wearing a swimsuit and shorts, Mr. R was working in his garden. He said he had tomatoes for my mom, so I followed him to his back porch. Then he told me how beautiful I had become, how gorgeous my body was, as he put the tomatoes in a bag and turned to me. Instead of handing me the bag, he pulled me to himself. With one arm holding me against him, he slipped his other hand inside my bathing suit and moaned.

Terrified, I realized I was in trouble. This time something was different, more intense and leading somewhere that frightened me like never before. Somehow, I broke free from his grip, grabbed the bag of tomatoes, and ran home.

I was still upset when I got there. I ran to my room, flung myself on the bed crying, and wondered where my life was heading. I was alone; no one cared what was happening to me. I felt like I was sinking into a deep darkness and there was no way out.

The following day was a Sunday. I was in my room when my sister called up the stairs, "Lisa, you have a visitor." After bounding downstairs, I peeked through the crack in the door and could barely make out a man in a suit on our front steps. I jumped from the landing to the front door, thinking my dad had stopped by after church. But on the other side of the locked screen door, to my horror, stood Mr. R.

For a second, I wondered if he had spent his morning in church devising plans for me. His car was in the driveway; he hadn't even been home yet. There he stood in his suit with his hands against the door frame and his face pressed to the screen, asking me to go somewhere with him. What a paralyzing development. He had never come to my house before.

Frozen in fear, I realized this could be the day that my life would end, one way or another. He was talking, but I couldn't comprehend his words. All I heard him say was, "I want you to come with me." My mind exploded with thoughts of what was about to happen. Everything I had feared from the day before was coming true.

Hero Joe

Suddenly, my sister's boyfriend stood between me and the screen door. Joe was a friend of mine. We had gone to elementary school together. He was almost as small as me, barely five feet tall, but tough. On the day I needed him to be, he was a giant. At that moment, he was the only thing keeping my life from utter destruction.

In my frozen state, I didn't hear the words he was saying but I knew they were threatening. Mr. R spun and hustled to his car. Joe watched him leave, then turned to me and said, "He won't bother you again. But if he does, tell me and I'll protect you."

I stumbled back to my room with a flicker of hope as the word *protector* echoed in my head. Maybe my life wasn't over just yet.

Mr. R never touched me again.

Why Me?

"Why me?" is a common question asked by abuse victims. While I can't say specifically why you or I had to suffer abuse, I can give you some general answers.

First, sin is a part of the world we live in. Christians are not going to be unaffected by the sin that is all around us and the depravity in every human being. If not for God restraining evil, we would all suffer much more than we do.

Paul wrote to Timothy, "But understand this, that in the last days there will come times of difficulty. For people will be lovers of self, lovers of money, proud, arrogant, abusive, disobedient to their parents, ungrateful, unholy, heartless, unappeasable, slanderous, without self-control, brutal, not loving good, treacherous, reckless, swollen with conceit, lovers of pleasure rather than lovers of God, having the appearance of godliness but denying its power. … Indeed, all who desire to live a godly life in Christ Jesus will be persecuted, while evil people and impostors will go on from bad to worse, deceiving and being deceived" (2 Timothy 3:1–4, 12–13). Our world is under the curse of sin and will only get worse until Christ comes again.

Second Corinthians 1 says that we suffer so that we can comfort others. It also says that through affliction we share in Christ's sufferings: "Blessed be the God and Father of our Lord Jesus Christ, the Father of mercies and God of all comfort, who comforts us in all our affliction, so that we may be able to comfort those who are in any affliction, with the comfort with which we ourselves are comforted by God. For as we share abundantly in Christ's sufferings, so through Christ, we share abundantly in comfort too" (vv. 3–5). What a blessing it is to be able to empathize with someone going through difficult circumstances, to be there when they need someone to cry with or pray with, and to guide them through the healing process. We may even have the privilege of being the conduit God uses to bring them to salvation.

When we comfort others, in a sense we are glorifying God by doing the good works he prepared us to do (Ephesians 2:10). That is the essence of Romans 8:28. The working of all things together for "good" is lived out when we take the trials of our lives and use the lessons learned to help others. Just by sharing your story and living an abundant, joy-filled life, you will demonstrate hope to someone who thought there was no possibility of overcoming their past.

In addition to helping others, suffering also shapes our character. Your parents may have used the line "it builds character" when they stuck you with some arduous chore. What they were really saying was that when you stick with something and see it through, you'll learn patience, perseverance, problem solving, accomplishment, confidence, and a host of other positive character traits. In a spiritual sense, suffering does the same thing: "More than that, we rejoice in our sufferings, knowing that suffering produces endurance, and endurance produces character, and character produces hope" (Romans 5:3 RSV).

What? Hope is born from suffering? Yes, suffering causes us to lean on God. It grows our faith and matures us. We can't have hope without complete trust in God, and suffering drives us to him. While shaping our character, suffering also refines us, making us a better reflection of Jesus.

Here's a beautiful story that illustrates this:

Malachi 3:3 says, "He will sit as a refiner and purifier of silver." This verse puzzled some women in a Bible study, and they wondered what this statement meant about the character and nature of God. One of the women offered to find out the process of refining silver and get back to the group at their next Bible study. That week, the woman called a silversmith and made an appointment to watch him at work. She didn't mention anything about the reason for her interest beyond her curiosity about the process of refining silver.

As she watched the silversmith, he held a piece of silver over the fire and let it heat up. He explained that in refining silver, one needed to hold the silver in the middle of the fire where the flames were hottest as to burn away all the impurities. The woman thought about God holding us in such a hot spot then she thought again about the verse that says: "He sits as a refiner and purifier of silver."

She asked the silversmith if it was true that he had to sit there in front of the fire the whole time the silver was being refined. The man answered that yes, he not only had to sit there holding the silver, but he had to keep his eyes on the silver the entire time it was in the fire. If the silver was left a moment too long in the flames, it would be destroyed. The woman was silent for a moment. Then she asked the silversmith, "How do you know when the silver is fully refined?" He smiled at her and answered, "Oh, that's easy—when I see my image in it."

If today you are feeling the heat of the fire, remember that God has His eye on you and will keep watching you until He sees His image in you. The refiner's fire will burn off whatever impurities keep us from reflecting his image.[1] That is powerful. It causes me to be thankful for the refiner's fire in my life, even though the time spent

in the fire is painful and leaves some scars. In the end,
if my life reflects his image, I can truly be thankful for
the suffering.

We'd like to think that all will go well for God's people, without times of pain. Verses like Jeremiah 29:11 are often taken out of context: "For I know the plans I have for you, declares the Lord, plans for your welfare and not for evil, to give you a future and a hope." We can be assured that God does have a plan for our lives, and it is a good plan. But that plan may, and in most cases does, include a time of suffering.

If you back up a few verses, you'll find that this promise of God is given after he tells Israel that they will suffer seventy years of exile. God tells them to build houses, live in them, marry, and raise families—because they will be there a long time. He even tells them to pray for the city where they are exiled. After all of that, we read, "For thus says the LORD: When seventy years are completed for Babylon, I will visit you, and I will fulfill to you my promise and bring you back to this place" (Jeremiah 29:10).

So the plan, the future and hope that God promises, comes after a long period of difficulty. In that seventy-year span, we can assume there were many people in exile who didn't live long enough to come back to the land and see the promise fulfilled. That doesn't change God's promise or plan for them. It didn't change that there was a future and a hope for them. They could still live their lives full of hope, trusting God for their future, whether that future included coming home to the land he promised them or coming home to him. Either way, their future was assured.

Finally, consider this quote from Charles Spurgeon:

He whose life is one even and smooth path will see but little of the glory of the Lord, for he has few occasions of self-emptying and hence but little fitness for being filled with the revelation of God. They who navigate little streams and shallow creeks know but little of the God of tempests. … Thank God, then, if you have been led by a rough road: it is this that has given you your experience of God's greatness and loving-kindness. Your troubles have enriched you with a wealth of knowledge to be gained by no other means. Your trials have been the crevice of the rock in which Jehovah has set you, as He did His servant Moses, that you might behold His glory as it passed by. Praise God that you have not been left to the darkness and ignorance that continued prosperity might have involved, but that in the great fight of affliction you have been qualified for the outshinings of His glory in His wonderful dealings with you. [2]Part of God's good plan for you was taking you through times of affliction, that you might have the privilege of beholding his glory that wouldn't happen any other way. In finding freedom from your past, you will also learn to praise God for *all* of your experiences. And that praise will be from your heart, genuinely thankful and amazed at the glory he has revealed to you.

Are you willing to allow God to use your suffering to help others? Maybe not yet, but as you find healing, ask God to provide opportunities to minister to others who have suffered in the same way.

CHAPTER 6:

Breaking the Grip of Darkness

Hero Teacher

Beginning high school was scary. I was already fearful and shy, so moving to a school of over two thousand students was terrifying. Sophomore orientation provided a little bit of comfort. We did a walk-through of the first day of school, navigating the hallways and finding our classrooms among the maze of pods. I memorized the route, feeling less than confident that I wouldn't get lost.

That first day arrived, and the hallways were so much more crowded than at orientation. My locker and homeroom were in a far corner of the school, as far as they could be from my first class. How was I going to make it across the school in the three and a half minutes before the late bell rang? I was late for my first class. The teacher was not happy. Neither was I.

The end-of-class bell rang, and the race was on to the next class. I made it in plenty of time and took a seat near the front. Geometry. Ugh, math. The teacher seemed friendly, at least nicer than the wicked English teacher I just escaped from. He was on the small size, the stereotypical math nerd but friendly.

The class period ended. I survived the first day of Geometry. The rest of my first day went about the same—sprinting to classes, pushed along by the throngs of students, searching for room numbers. Typing, Biology, lunch, Spanish, Psychology. Day one of high school was in the books. Time to study the map for day two.

Day two went a little better. As Geometry class ended, I gathered my books and headed for the door. I was at the end of the line of students jumping into the flow of traffic in the hallway. As I waited my turn to make the leap, the math teacher said, "Have a good day, Boom-Boom." No one had called me that since elementary school (only my fifth-grade teacher used it). I spun around to see my math teacher leaning on his desk with a huge grin on his face. He laughed. "Gotcha!"

"How did you know my nickname?" I asked.

"Mr. Knight is my best friend. We have a lawn mowing business together in the summer. He knew his first class would be starting high school this year and asked if I had any of you. When I said your name, he responded with the nickname he had given you and told me to use it and see what you did."

All the sudden, I had a trusting connection with this teacher. I couldn't really picture the two men as best friends. This teacher seemed like he would have been the captain of the chess club, while Mr. Knight seemed more suited to be captain of the baseball team. But maybe he played chess too. They were friends, and to me they were heroes. From that moment in his classroom, I had a friend in a nerdy Geometry teacher.

Not long into the school year, one of the boys in class became irritated with something and got in the teacher's face in a threatening manner. He was bigger than the teacher and behaving very aggressively, but the teacher didn't back away. He forced the angry student right out of the room, taking charge of the situation and his classroom. Then he went back to what he had been teaching without even a quiver in his voice.

I was impressed. The nerdy math teacher had a tough, fearless side. He proved to be someone I could trust, another man God used to show me the good, gentle side of men who could be tough when needed.

Once a Villain, Always a Villain

I never took a bus to school. Our home was just a mile from the high school, so I didn't qualify for bus transportation. That was okay with me. I never wanted to deal with bus rides with all the other kids. But in high school, anyone involved in after-school activities could take the late bus home, even if they didn't normally ride a bus.

I usually walked home from school, but after a meeting, my friends were taking the late bus, so I decided to take it too. We were talking and laughing as we waited to board the bus. But when I looked up as the bus door opened, there in the driver's seat was Mr. R. He smiled at me and welcomed me onto the bus.

I thought about getting off and walking home, but my friends were with me. I did a quick mental survey of the kids on the bus and where they lived. It made sense that I would be the first one dropped off, so I boarded the bus and sat in the back with my friends.

It didn't take me long to realize the bus was taking the opposite route. My fears escalated as one by one my friends departed, finally leaving me alone on the bus. I remained planted in the seat at the back of the bus. Mr. R was taunting me, telling me what he was going to do. How was I going to get off the bus safely? How could I get past him?

The bus turned onto my street. I craned my neck, searching my front porch and driveway for any sign of my sister or her boyfriend. No one. The house and driveway were empty. What now?

Hero Neighbor

The bus came to a stop. Mr. R beckoned me to come to him. I started down the aisle, my mind racing. Maybe I could get past him. He unbuckled his seatbelt. Just as I reached the front seats, my next-door neighbor came out of his house. He had his own business but drove a bus part time. He recognized Mr. R and called to him with a friendly wave. When Mr. R turned toward him, I bolted out the door. They chatted for a few seconds, and I didn't look back.

God had done it again. Just at the moment I needed a rescuer, he sent my neighbor. Had it been someone else, maybe Mr. R wouldn't have been distracted. And why was the neighbor home at that time of day? He usually wasn't. The answer was obvious: God intervened and used my neighbor, without the man even knowing it, to save a terrified young girl.

For the next two summers, I worked at the pool. Mr. R was a frequent visitor. Every time I was alone at the front desk when he arrived, he would lean on the counter, making comments about my breasts and how much he wanted to touch them. By this time, I was a different person. He didn't scare me anymore. I told him to get lost. After he disappeared through the door into the men's locker room, I couldn't help but wonder who he was there to victimize. But my time was over.

Out of Darkness, Light

Not long after my last encounter with Mr. R, God intervened in my life through a tragedy. Though I had attended church all my life, I really didn't know God personally, not as *my* Savior and Lord. I knew a lot about him, but he wasn't a part of my everyday life.

Being a part of the senior high youth group at our church was fun. My life was improving in every area. Then just as life was going so well, our twenty-one-year-old youth leader was killed in a car accident. I was furious with God. How could he do this? Jim had so much to offer.

As I cried and lashed out at God, a clear, quiet voice spoke to my heart: "What more could he have done? Everything he did, he did for me." I realized I was not living for Christ, even though I claimed to be his. I asked God to forgive me for my sin and help me to live a life that would honor him. Everything changed at that moment. I had peace in my heart for the first time in my life.

I devoured God's Word, reading late into the night. The psalms were especially powerful and comforting to me. Psalms 40 and 71 speak of God as a rescuer and protector: "The LORD … heard my cry. He drew me up from the pit of destruction" (Psalm 40:1–2), and "Rescue me, O my God, from the hand of the wicked, from the grasp of the unjust and cruel man" (Psalm 71:4). A protector, a rescuer, a Savior—the very things I had dreamed about. In the pages of Scripture, my heart began to heal. Fear and doubt were replaced with peace and rest. In Christ, I found freedom from my past.

As I began to understand my new life in Christ, I learned that my old self was crucified with him. It had been put to death and no longer had any power over me. The cross of Christ was a turning point. I saw that it wasn't just my *sin* that the cross had expunged, but all of my *past*. I truly was made new. I was not in any way bound to my past. Jesus had set me free, and I was free indeed.

Have you trusted Jesus as your Savior? Acts 4:12 tells us, "And there is salvation in no one else; for there is no other name under heaven that has been given among men by which we must be saved." Apart from salvation, it is impossible to have any power over sin. And while the world can offer you ways to cope with your past, you will not find true freedom from it unless it has been put to death. That only happens in Jesus who died and rose again so that we also can have new life.

My favorite words in the Bible are *but God*. Those two little words change everything. We were dead in our sins, *but God* made us alive with Christ (Ephesians 2:1–7). Our flesh and our heart may fail, *but God* is the strength of our heart forever (Psalm 73:26). We were afflicted at every turn, *but God*, who comforts the downcast, comforted us (2 Corinthians 7:5–7). My life has been a chorus of *but God*s. He has taken a broken, abused heart and breathed into it new life full of joy and wholeness.

Hero Friend

When I was saved at sixteen, I sought out Christian friends. I already had some good friends at church. Joining the local Young Life club opened up a world of new friends at my high school.

My closest friend was Alan, a boy I had known all my life. We lived a block apart and went to the same elementary school, junior high, and senior high. We also attended the same church, where we both were involved in the choir and youth group, and even had birthdays just nine days apart.

Alan had always been a friend, but as my new faith started to grow, he became my go-to guy. I could tell him anything and ask him anything, and, most of all, I could trust him. I was struggling with understanding some things about myself, my past, and about God. When I felt overwhelmed by it all, I'd call Alan.

We would walk around our neighborhood for hours, talking through my issues and questions. He had been saved longer than I had, and he had a good understanding of God's Word. He helped me work through some difficult things and taught me to trust God, that His plan is good. The love and kindness he showed me during my teenage years were invaluable, and I am so thankful God used him in my life.

Even today, when I'm going through a trial, I want to see Alan. He lives outside Boston, so I can't just call him up and go for a walk. We visit a few times a year as I pass through Massachusetts on trips to Maine. And I can always count on him to answer text messages right away.

His eyes seem to pierce right through me when he asks, "How are you doing?" It's not the typical "how are you" question. He truly wants to know and waits for a complete answer. His hugs remain the best, strong and just a second or two longer than most.

Back in high school, people thought that Alan and I were dating. We were always together. I helped him shop for clothes, and he gave me rides to school before I started driving. We were inseparable. But we never dated. He did have a huge influence on my dating life though. It was through Alan that I met my wonderful husband, who happens to be his cousin.

CHAPTER 7:

Freeing My Mind

Over the next year, my life experienced an extreme make-over. Everything about it changed. "Therefore, if anyone is in Christ, he is a new creation. The old has passed away. Behold, the new has come" (2 Corinthians 5:17) became so real to me.

My personality went from being fearful and shy to fearless and outgoing. I tried new things—things I didn't think I could do, everything from rock climbing to student government. I became an officer in our church youth group and was eager to share with my peers how God changed my life. And I caught the attention of a handsome young man.

Doug was the cool guy in our church youth group. He played guitar, sang solos, and was the best at everything. He also was the best-looking guy around, with a mop of dark curls and a powerfully square jaw. I never thought he was looking at me too. There were lots of other girls, more popular than I was, who longed to date him. (Besides, he thought I was dating Alan.)

While on a youth group trip to my family's cabin in Maine, he and I started hanging out together, mostly because we were both with Alan, which put us with each other. We spent the week canoeing, hiking, swimming, and enjoying each other's company. He was such a gentleman, lending me his jacket on a cool night while stargazing. Later in the week, he caught me when my foot slipped during a particularly challenging hike. Truly my hero.

When we returned to our regular lives, I noticed Doug put some distance between us, and I asked him about it. Had I read him wrong? Was our attraction just a youth-group-trip thing? I saw him one afternoon in the high school cafeteria and decided it was time to find out what was going on.

"Can I talk to you?" I asked and pulled him aside from the group of Young Life kids he was chatting with. "Maybe I misunderstood, but I felt like we had a made a connection in Maine. But you seem to be backing off. Was I wrong? Is there a problem?"

He flashed his killer smile and said, "No, you're not wrong. I really like you and would really like to date you. But I've made a commitment to Young Life to be a club leader for this school year. I need to honor that. Since you're a Young Life kid, we can't date right now. If you'd be willing to wait a year, I would love to start a deeper relationship with you then."

It wasn't a difficult choice. I already knew he was the man of my dreams, the kind of man I once thought I would *never* find. What was one year?

Hero Leader

This hero is really two people, but I rarely think of them separately, always as a couple. Tim and Amy Sharadin were the Young Life leaders at my high school. They became my good friends too. Tim was a man who made me feel very safe. He was what I always imagined a big brother would be like, joking around a lot but also giving the sense that he was watching out for me.

Tim was always happy to see me and always had time to talk. That was part of his role as a Young Life leader, to strike up conversations with kids, but it was also very genuine. He really cared about each kid who he encountered. At the end of a school day, I always knew when Tim was sitting in the lobby of the high school, engaging students, because I could hear his laugh bouncing off the hallway walls.

Tim taught Campaigners, the Young Life Bible study, which met at Doug's house. Although my motivations for going every Monday night were probably not always pure, God used Tim's teaching from the Word to grow my faith. I remember him saying, "You have to cultivate God's Word in your heart." Then he explained what it means to cultivate something—to break up the ground, plant seeds, water them, care for them, and finally harvest what's been planted. That's what I needed to do with God's Word for it to take root and bear fruit in my life.

His wife, Amy, was the epitome of a role model for young women. She had a quiet confidence about her and an unshakable faith. Amy was a loving wife and mother, and welcomed teens into her home without the slightest fear of the damage they could cause. (At least, she didn't show any fear.) She also tempered Tim's crazy side, shaking her head while laughing at his antics. They truly loved people, especially teenagers, and entered my life at a crucial time. My years of abuse had just ended, and I was a brand-new Christian.

Through their ministry, I learned who God was, how to study the Bible, and how to pray. They laid a solid foundation in my new faith and life. As a new believer, I was scared to death to read or pray aloud in a group. But their example and encouragement helped me to get more comfortable and grow in those areas. They took us one step at a time, starting with "popcorn" prayers of just one line to help us get comfortable with praying aloud. Then we'd pray for two things, and before long I could pray confidently in a group setting.

It was during a Young Life trip to Colorado one summer that things really changed for me. Because I was challenged and sometimes forced to do things I never would have tried before, I gained confidence. When I was successful at things I didn't think I could do, my attitude changed. By the end of our weeklong trip, I was a new, confident person. It took a high-ropes course to get there, but I was able to break through all the fear of my past and begin again.

Once Doug and I started dating, we spent a lot of time with Tim and Amy. They modeled the Christian family for us. Without knowing it, they became our mentors in trusting God's plan, in youth ministry, and in parenting. They continue to fulfill that role, and I am so thankful to have these godly examples in my life.

As it turned out, the year of waiting to date Doug was a time of spiritual growth and study in God's Word, learning about God's design for relationships and sex. If I had started dating at that time, my past would have played a much bigger and more damaging role in our relationship. My desire for a physical relationship was much stronger because of what I had already been exposed to. By the time Doug and I started dating, I was in a much healthier place both spiritually and emotionally.

It's All in Your Mind

So much of the struggle really is in our mind. We need to saturate it with Scripture, which will in turn change our thinking. We do that by following what Scripture says, dwelling on things above: "Set your minds on the things that are above, not on things that are on earth. For you have died, and your life is hidden with Christ in God" (Colossians 3:2–3).

If you're not sure how to do this, start by asking yourself if what you're thinking lines up with Philippians 4:8: "Whatever is true, whatever is honorable, whatever is just, whatever is pure, whatever is lovely, whatever is commendable, if there is any excellence, if there is anything worthy of praise, think about these things." Training the mind in Scripture changes the heart. The brain is amazing. How it works is fascinating. How does your brain know that someone's name starts with a K but it can't come up with the rest of the name—until three a.m.?

Brain development in children can be greatly affected by trauma. The very personhood (the development of the mind, emotions, and spirit) of a victim of childhood sexual abuse is at risk. Abuse can cause them to mentally shut down. Maybe their way of dealing with what happened was to go somewhere else in their mind or to create an alternate personality. How they think was damaged by the lies they were told. What was real and what wasn't became blurred. How they feel and relate to others is directly linked to how they think.

Even so, the brain can be rewired. This is why it's so important to renew our minds through God's Word, the Truth that will set us free: "Do not be conformed to this world, but be transformed by the renewing of your mind" (Romans 12:2). Salvation doesn't just affect your heart, it also affects your mind. In fact, your heart will follow where your mind leads it. In the mind is where we have understanding and discernment. You may have heard people talk about having head knowledge but not heart knowledge. What they're saying is that the truth of God's Word hasn't caused a change in their behavior.

But change is possible when we seek to understand Scripture. You'll never hear someone say that they have heart knowledge but not head knowledge. You may hear of those who follow their heart instead of their head, but that doesn't usually end well. Without discernment, our hearts can be deceived, so everything we believe needs to be thought through. The renewing of our minds is vital to understanding Scripture and changing our behavior to be more like Christ.

Again, we can turn to Romans 8 to understand more about the importance of our minds in our spiritual lives: "For those who live according to the flesh set their minds on the things of the flesh, but those who live according to the Spirit set their minds on the things of the Spirit. For to set the mind on the flesh is death, but to set the mind on the Spirit is life and peace" (vv. 5–6).

Life and peace—isn't that what we all desire? To find it, we need to set our minds on spiritual things and not earthly things. The spiritual things are not high, lofty thoughts but the everyday things of the Christian life. We should be thinking about how we can help someone in need, where we can use our gifts to benefit others, and who we can encourage.

Consider the fruit of the Spirit in Galatians 5: love, joy, peace, patience, kindness, goodness, faithfulness, gentleness, and self-control. These are the "things of the Spirit" upon which we should set our minds. Think through them. How can you demonstrate these things in your life? It won't look the same for everyone, but it will always be in relationship with others. Once we set our minds on these things, then we can act and *do* the things of the Spirit that bring life and peace. That is how head knowledge becomes heart knowledge.

The Bible has numerous passages that exhort Christians to be of one mind or the same mind. For example, 1 Peter 3:8 says, "Finally, all of you, have unity of mind, sympathy, brotherly love, a tender heart, and a humble mind." This passage sounds somewhat like one on the fruit of the Spirit, but it is written for relationships within the church.

People who take this to heart don't think more highly of themselves than they ought. They seek unity at the cost of their own desires or opinions, and the unity comes from how they think. The importance of thinking Biblically for the individual Christian and the body of Christ cannot be overstated.

CHAPTER 8:

Free to Love

Hero Husband

Doug was everything I had hoped a boyfriend would be. He opened car doors, set up romantic dates, and treated me like a princess. We spent hours reading God's Word, praying, taking long walks, and getting to know each other. He even wrote songs for me and sung them to me in his beautiful baritone voice. It was more wonderful than I could have imagined.

I was so thankful to God for bringing us together and for making us wait. Our romance was the first one for each of us. How special and blessed we are to be each other's first everything. Almost a month after our first date, he kissed me. Not only was it the sweetest kiss in the history of the world, but it was also the first kiss for either of us, something we still celebrate every December 23. I had found love—a strong, grounded, forever love. My heart was so full. I couldn't wait to marry him.

When the time came in our relationship for me to tell him about my past abuse, he didn't run away. In fact, he became very protective of me. At the time, I was working for a company, and one night I was there late, trying to get a project done. This was back in the days when an office computer took up an entire room and you had to go into the room to use it. The company's owner was getting ready to lock up and saw my car outside, so he came looking for me.

When he came into the computer room, I said, "Just a few more minutes and I'll be done. Can you wait?" He replied, "Well, there's no one here but the two of us. I can wait as long as you want." He moved closer and put his hand on my shoulder. "In fact, you should stop by my office before you leave." His hand moved to my hair as he leaned over and breathed in its fragrance.

For a moment I was paralyzed. But he left, and I quickly finished the job, gathered my things, and left. I didn't stop at his office, instead shouting that I was leaving as I walked out the front door.

I was a little shaken by the incident, and when I saw Doug later that night, I told him what had happened. He calmed me down and assured me that he would do everything in his power to keep me safe.

The next day, I was called into the boss's office. To my shock, Doug was there, dressed in a suit and with his Bible in hand. Apparently, he'd had a talk with my boss, who was a professing Christian. My boss apologized and promised it wouldn't happen again. And it didn't. The idea that I had a protector here in the flesh was almost more than I could believe. I thanked God for his goodness to me in providing this wonderful man.

After dating for about two years, Doug asked my mother if he could have my hand in marriage. It was very romantic, except that she said no. She believed we were too young. I was only nineteen at the time, and she told him to come back in six months. He did, but she again said no.

This time I asked her, "Why are you refusing to give us permission to be engaged?" She said, "Doug is too much like your father." What? That was it? I couldn't believe it at the time, but I suppose that was true. They both were quiet, gentle, musically gifted men. I had a very good opinion of my father. She did not. In fact, she put him in the villain category. She was sure my marriage to Doug would end the same way hers had, in heartache and raising children by myself.

She asserted, "You don't know how difficult it is to raise children alone." I protested, "I don't plan on raising children alone." She retorted, "Neither did I."

Nothing I could say would change her mind. I tried to point out how different they really were—and how different she and I were. But she was not convinced. Even so, we were determined to honor her by accepting her decision, and we continued dating and planning for marriage, whenever that would come.

Doug waited another six months, and by then my mother was ready to say yes. I think the love and kindness Doug showed her during that time of waiting won her over.

Our wedding day finally arrived. What a glorious day! The weather for our outdoor reception was perfect. The flowers were beautiful. All the plans had come together, and it was time. Just before we started down the aisle, I reminded my dad not to step on my dress (remember, he was a klutz). Throughout the day, I couldn't stop smiling. My face hurt, but I just couldn't stop. Before we knew it, the day was over and off we went to begin a life full of joy, love, and commitment.

Our honeymoon was a happy time. We were still smiling as we drove away from the reception, and it felt almost unreal that we were actually married. One of the most annoying things about dating was needing to go home at the end of a long, tiring day. I was so happy that those days were over. We could end our day together and wake up the next morning together—still one of my favorite things after thirty-three years of marriage.

We had some apprehension going into our wedding night. Though we were pretty sure our physical relationship would be fine, it would be a new experience in a lot of ways. I couldn't help wondering if memories would ruin it. Fortunately, it was a wonderful night, and the reality of falling asleep in my husband's arms was even sweeter than I had dreamed.

Intimacy

A lot of sexual abuse victims who marry have issues with intimacy. This is usually due to the memories and feelings that come flooding back when they are touched in an intimate way. At those times, the best way to conquer such feelings is to remind yourself of the gospel. That's right, the gospel of Jesus Christ. Why? Because the gospel is the good news that Jesus came into the world to save people from sin.

That saving power comes with loads of benefits. Jesus says he came to give life abundantly: "The thief comes only to steal and kill and destroy. I came that they may have life and have it abundantly" (John 10:10). Paul says, "For freedom Christ has set us free; stand firm therefore, and do not submit again to a yoke of slavery" (Galatians 5:1). Freedom is yours in Jesus. Stand firm in that freedom.

Marriage is a beautiful picture of the relationship between Jesus and his bride, the church. Of course, Satan wants to destroy that imagery. He wants to use the memories from your past to destroy you and keep you from the beautiful fulfillment God has for you within your marriage relationship. Jesus wants you to have freedom in him and an abundant life.

When your mind and your memories go to destructive places, refocus your mind (yes, in the middle of intimacy with your spouse) to who you are in Jesus and what He has done for you. Tell yourself, *I am a child of the King. Nothing has power over me, and my past has no place in my life now.* Then think about this wonderful spouse who God has put in your life to walk this path with you. Focus on your spouse's touch and what they feel like, not the feelings associated with memories. Doing those things will help you enjoy the abundant life He has given you, in purity and beauty.

This may not happen all at once. Or it may be great for a while and then out of nowhere, Satan tries to bind you again. So be prepared, have a battle plan, and trust that God has already won the war. You just need to trust Him.

Galatians 2:20 says, "I have been crucified with Christ. It is no longer I who live, but Christ who lives in me. And the life that I now live in the flesh, I live by faith in the Son of God, who loved me and gave himself for me." By faith in what Jesus has done for us, we can leave our past nailed to the cross, blotted out by Christ. It's dead. Dead things have no control, no power. The ugliness of sexual abuse *can* be put in the past, hidden in Christ with God. "For you have died, and your life is hidden with Christ in God" (Colossians 3:3). You *can* have the abundant life, including in your sex life, that Jesus promised.

It's All Good

Only a few weeks into our marriage, I started to feel a little queasy now and then. Nothing serious, it seemed to be triggered by certain smells. Then I started having a craving for olives and was repulsed by bagels. Weird. After a few more weeks, we knew I was pregnant.

Being a mother was all I ever wanted to be. I still have my first-grade story on what I wanted to be when I grew up. Written on one of those extra-wide pages with space at the top to draw a picture and lines at the bottom for writing the story, it reads, *I want to be a mother. That is all.* My pregnancy was a dream come true. We were thrilled and couldn't wait to share the news with family and friends.

Doug's parents and my dad and stepmother were ecstatic. My mom was less than enthusiastic. She behaved as though it was something to be ashamed of, like the pregnancy was unwanted. "You should have waited until you were financially secure," she said. "Don't you dare put that baby in a daycare center." She told no one about my pregnancy, and although she didn't exactly say it, I could read her thoughts: *I knew this would happen. You're gonna end up just like me.*

I had no intention of using daycare. In fact, at about six months pregnant, I left my job to prepare for the baby and become a full-time wife and mother. As my belly grew, my mother's heart softened. She had never been pregnant (both my sister and I are adopted). She seemed in awe the first time she felt the baby kick her hand through my tummy. From that point on, she was on board.

After what seemed like way more than nine months, we welcomed our first son into our lives. Although he was late, he came in a hurry on the day he arrived. He was perfect and looked just like his daddy. Could life get any better?

Life was truly wonderful. I was a stay-at-home mom, and Doug was working as an operating room nurse at our local hospital. We had found a church home and were ministering there in the youth group and the music ministry. I was so thankful to God for the way he was orchestrating my life. Yes, it started out with some bad notes, but it was evolving into a beautiful symphony.

Just before our son's first birthday, we bought our first house and settled into suburban family life. Doug went to work, enjoyed gardening, and played Legos with our little boy. I stayed at home, taking care of our son, baking cookies, teaching Bible studies, and loving my life. My past was so far removed that it almost seemed like it had happened to someone else.

But it was about to come back like a sudden trumpet blast into my sublime symphony—and remain there for years to come.

CHAPTER 9:

Slipping the Grip of My Past

Unexpected Return

Three years into married life, I joined a group of women from our church for a retreat. We had a great time, laughing and learning together. One of the speakers talked about forgiving people from your past and letting go of resentments, and after her session I spoke to two of the ladies on the trip about my past. It was the first time I talked to anyone except for my husband about my abuse.

They listened and were sympathetic. But they told me, "If that man is ever arrested, you'll have to tell your story." I said, "That will never happen. It's been nearly ten years since my abuse ended, and he hasn't been caught yet so it's not likely he'll ever be caught."

We returned home Sunday night, and before seven a.m. on Monday morning, my phone rang. I dragged myself out of bed in a post-retreat stupor. The caller was one of the women I had confided in at the retreat. Why was she calling so early, and why did morning people have to bother the rest of us? I tried to focus on what she was saying.

She asked, "Was the man who abused you named Mr. R?" I said, "Yes, how do you know that?" Her reply made my head swirl and my knees weaken, but I was now wide awake: "He's been arrested. It's in the paper." I sunk to the floor in disbelief. She finished, "You know you have to talk to the police."

I told her I would, hung up the phone, and dissolved into a puddle of tears. How could this be happening now? My life was perfect. It was all I ever wanted. Why did I need to deal with this now?

My husband, who had been enjoying his bowl of cereal and was unaware of the other end of the phone conversation, dropped his spoon in his bowl and picked me up off the floor. I relayed the conversation through choked sobs. He suggested I call our pastor's wife for advice, but it was much too early in the morning to make any phone calls, so I said goodbye to my husband as he went to work, and then sat down with my Bible.

Turning to the Bible study I was planning to start that day, I read about how we suffer so that we can comfort others who are suffering in the same way with the comfort we have received from God (2 Corinthians 1:4 paraphrased). *What, Lord?* I thought. *Oh no, I can't share this ugliness with others. I don't want this to be the thing you use in me. It needs to stay hidden. There are plenty of other things, other lessons I have learned, other experiences you can use, but not this one.*

Fighting with God is futile. Really, the fight was only on my side of the conversation. God said all he planned to say in his Word and waited for me to hear it. I knew in my heart, even before the argument began, how it would end. So, with a lot of fear in my heart and butterflies the size of Godzilla in my stomach, I said, "God, if this is the purpose for what I've suffered, guide my steps and give me strength to do what you have planned for me."

Three hours later I was sitting in the living room of our pastor's home, pouring out my story to his wife. She sat in stunned silence.

Literally, her mouth was hanging open. The only words she had said (over and over) during my story were, "Oh, my stars." When I finished, she said, "I can't believe it. You're so together, so normal, so full of joy. How could you have gone through this and turned out okay?"

I told her that when I was saved, I believed God took away not only my sins but also my past, and that had rendered it powerless, hidden with Christ.

She was amazed, having counseled so many women whose lives were in ruins because of similar abuse. She also confirmed what my other friend had said. The police need to know my story, if only to establish a pattern of behavior that might help their case.

Stuck

Some victims get completely "stuck" in their past. They just can't move on. When this happens, it's time to do some serious heart searching. Like David, ask God to show you your heart, and if there is something there that is keeping you from experiencing freedom from your past, confess it and ask God to remove it far from you.

Some people get stuck on purpose. They seem to have a need to live in crisis. It could be the attention it brings. It could be that it's just easier to live the way they always have. They may need to ask God to give them the *desire* to be free.

That's the idea behind Psalm 37:4: "Delight yourself in the LORD, and he will give you the desires of your heart." Rather than giving you what you desire, God gives you the desires you should have—his desires. The desire to always be in a crisis is not God's desire. But a desire to live an abundant life, free from the weight of your past, is certainly God's desire for you.

Sometimes people get stuck because they're simply too afraid to move. It's like the feeling of being in quicksand. You think that if you keep perfectly still, you'll be okay. But start moving or trying to get out of your predicament, and you'll be swallowed up. We've already talked about fear, the need to overcome it, and ways to be courageous, so I won't repeat that here. But if fear is keeping you from moving on, reread that chapter and ask God to show you what you're afraid of and how to overcome it.

Often, sexual abuse victims become stuck because they see themselves as sinful and unworthy of having an abundant life free from their past. This usually comes from the way their body reacted to the abuser, from being told by the abuser that they are the ones sinning—by tempting them or dressing provocatively, or from being told that they were a willing participant in the abuse or some other lie. (We will cover these things in chapter ten.) But to understand this point and get you unstuck, let's assume that there was some sin involved on your part.

Freedom from sin will not come without true repentance, which means turning from the sin that binds us. Sometimes turning from sin comes easily, but other times it's a struggle you face every day. But the more you choose not to sin, the easier it will become. There is never a valid excuse to remain in your sin. The Holy Spirit gives us the power to defeat sin. We need to acknowledge our sin, confess it, and turn away from it. Choosing not to sin is part of God's grace. Alistair Begg put it this way: "As a result of grace, we have been saved from sin's penalty. One day we will be saved from sin's presence. In the meantime, we are being saved from sin's power." [3]

One false belief that keeps people stuck is that God's forgiveness isn't enough. We may say that we believe God has forgiven us, but we can't forgive ourselves. This is not only absurd but it's also not biblical. We will not find the idea of forgiving ourselves anywhere in Scripture, no matter how hard we search. That is because only God can forgive sin—and only God *needs* to forgive our sin. Sin is falling short of his glory, missing the mark of his required perfection. We can fall a little bit short or fall short by a mile, but any level of falling short is sin, and a price needs to be paid to cover that sin. That is what Jesus did for us. He paid the price of our sin by going to the cross as a perfect sacrifice, having never fallen short of God's glory. We can have confidence in God's forgiveness because of his acceptance of Jesus' sacrifice, not because of anything in us.

Often, our sin against God involves people. There are times we need to ask other people to forgive us or to offer forgiveness to another person. Even so, people can't forgive our *sin*. The forgiveness they offer is to choose not to hold our sin against us, to behave as if it never happened, and to have a restored relationship. As Christians, it is our duty to have a heart ready to forgive. Jesus indicated this in the Lord's Prayer when he said, "forgive us as we forgive our debtors."

If we desire and seek God's forgiveness, we must also be ready and willing to forgive others. If they choose not to forgive us, it does not negate God's forgiveness. At that point, we are right with God. We do not need to keep seeking their forgiveness. It is their responsibility to forgive the first time we ask The same goes for us. If God has forgiven us, we are responsible to let go of that sin. When we choose not to move on, we are living in disobedience.

As well, when we say that we can't forgive ourselves, we put ourselves above God—not a place we want to be. That declares Jesus' sacrifice was not sufficient. What could possibly be deficient in Jesus' sacrifice? For us to offer ourselves forgiveness? How arrogant. If the perfect, sinless, all-powerful God forgives us, who are we to say that we can't forgive? It's just another of Satan's lies to keep us from the abundant life God has for us.

Read Romans 8. Verse 1 tells us that there is no condemnation for those who are in Christ. If you feel condemned, first ask yourself if you are in Christ. Have you asked Jesus to save you? Are you walking in obedience to God's Word? If you can say yes to those questions, then you are no longer condemned, you are free from your sin and your past. Consider John 8:31–32, 36: "So Jesus said to the Jews who had believed in him, 'If you abide in my word, you are truly my disciples, and you will know the truth, and the truth will set you free.' … So if the Son sets you free, you will be free indeed."

The end of Romans 8 gives an exhaustive list of all the things that cannot separate us from the love of God. Really, nothing can come between us and God except unbelief. Maybe that's what "forgiving ourselves" really is, unbelief that God can really accept us with all the baggage from our past. Unbelief will separate us from God because unbelief is sin, and sin is the only thing that can separate us from the love of God.

Think about the imagery Micah uses regarding our sin: "He will again have compassion on us. He will tread our iniquities underfoot. He will cast all our sins into the depths of the sea" (Micah 7:19). God's the one who crushes our sins and removes them so far from us they could never be a part of our lives again. Think about the depths of the sea. Man has been to the moon but not to the utter depths of the sea. We can't get there because the pressure at that depth would crush us. That's the image of what God has done with our sin—and along with it, our past. It is gone forever and cannot bubble to the surface.

Consider another example in the life of King David. After David sinned sexually with Bathsheba and then sinned again by having her husband killed to cover it up, he was confronted by the prophet Nathan: "David said to Nathan, 'I have sinned against the LORD.' And Nathan said to David, 'The Lord also has put away your sin … but the child shall die'" (2 Samuel 12:13–14). David then fasted and prayed until the child died, but then he arose, washed, and ate. The confession was over, the judgment was over, and the punishment was over, and David moved on, asking God to restore the joy of his salvation (Psalm 51). We have an advantage that David didn't: Jesus has taken the punishment for our sin on himself.

CHAPTER 10:

Freedom from Shame

Not Your Fault

The police were eager to talk to me. The day came, and the butterflies in my stomach took on a life of their own. I was pretty sure they were going to fly out my mouth. But when I got in my car, there was a note from my dear husband that quoted Philippians 4:6–7: "Be anxious for nothing but in everything by prayer and supplication, with thanksgiving, let your requests be made known to God. And the peace of God, which passes all understanding, will guard your hearts and your minds in Christ Jesus." It also said, *I love you.* A calm washed over me.

I met with two detectives, told them my story, answered a lot of questions, and then went through it again, this time while it was recorded. It was easier to tell the story to strangers in very matter-of-fact questions and answers. Still, it was strange and scary to say it out loud. Guilt and shame rose up from somewhere deep inside of me, and I started questioning myself because they asked questions like, "Did you do anything to encourage his behavior toward you?"

I had wrestled with that question my whole life. I said no, but I really wasn't convinced of that. After all, I had been wearing a figure-flattering swimsuit several times when around Mr. R. I knew he was attracted to me, and I may have even teased him, bending over to reveal a little more cleavage. But the fact was, at the time of the abuse I was between the ages of five and fifteen and he was an adult. That made him completely responsible for his actions, regardless of what I had done, said, or felt.

An adult who is not a pedophile would not be attracted to a child. He would walk away, would be responsible for the child's well-being, and would do the right thing. It would take a long time for me to really understand that and have complete freedom from shame. But it would come.

If you are reading this because you were a victim of childhood sexual abuse, here is the one thing to remember, even if everything else is forgotten when you close this book: *It was not your fault.*

A few days later, I returned to the police station to read the transcript of my story. It was so strange to see it, for the first time, written down. I signed the statement and returned home to wait for the trial to begin, not knowing if I would be called to testify.

Almost a year would pass before the trial began. Whenever I thought about facing him in a court room, fear welled up inside, almost choking me. Would I be able to even speak? The police called now and then to update me on how things were progressing. Other women had also come forward, but I was one of two they planned to use. The others' lives were in shambles, and their testimonies wouldn't be considered credible.

Since Mr. R's defense was his stellar character, they wanted a witness with an equally impressive character. I could completely understand why these other women couldn't keep their lives together. Except for God's grace in my life, I can only imagine what path I would have chosen. Like other abused women, would I have become sexually promiscuous? Would I have sought out other sexually fulfilling relationships? Would I have been completely turned off by any relationship with a man? Would I have turned to drugs or alcohol to numb the pain?

Fortunately, I don't know the answers to those questions because God pulled me out of the miry pit before I was consumed by the darkness.

Hero-In-Law

C. Lloyd Radcliff was my father-in-law, but my first memories of him are as the "old ladies" Sunday School teacher at church. As a youngster, I was a little afraid of him. He was intimidating. Not a big, imposing figure, but he was someone who commanded respect.

When I started dating his youngest son, I was a little nervous that Mr. Radcliff wouldn't approve. He was very old-school. He went to work from nine to five every day, and his wife stayed at home caring for the kids and house. They were very much a Cleaver-esque sort of household, only without the shenanigans.

It didn't seem to me that he would put up with shenanigans. I was from a single-parent home where things were loud and crazy. While both of our families are Pennsylvania Dutch, his was the traditional, stoic, unemotional sort, while mine was the noisy, laughing, hugging kind. When Doug was twenty years old, he received an award at church. His parents hugged him after the service, and Doug said it was the first time that his dad had ever hugged him. There was no turning back after that; Mr. Radcliff was a hugger.

I soon learned that he was a much softer man than I thought. My first realization came when I was at the Radcliff home for dinner.

Every night, he came home at six p.m. He walked through the door and, before saying a word to anyone, beelined to his wife and gave her a kiss. Maybe he wasn't so hard after all.

It turned out that he had a soft side for the girls in his life, me included. Our special connection came through our shared love of football, particularly the Philadelphia Eagles and Penn State Nittany Lions. We watched the 1982 NCAA Championship game together. Penn State came back in the fourth quarter to beat #1 Georgia. Dad and I leaped from our seats, cheering and hugging. I was in. He was now wrapped around my finger. In future years, when a great play happened during an Eagles or Penn State game, Dad would call me to talk about it, not his sons or grandsons, but his football soulmate.

Doug looks like his dad. In our early years of dating and marriage, I would often look at his dad and think, *That's what Doug will be like when he's older*, and it was a good thing. When the grandchildren came along, Dad became famous for his "bounce." He had just the right way of cradling and bouncing fussy babies that put them right to sleep. It often put Dad to sleep as well, but he always had a good grip on the babies.

On the day I went to the police station to tell them my story, Doug's mom watched our two-year-old son. I had told her what was going on, but I didn't feel comfortable talking about it with Dad. I wasn't sure how he would react. Men of his generation didn't talk about such things. But that morning, he was there when I dropped off my son. He gave me a big hug and said, "I love you. I'm proud of you. Anything you need, I will be here for you."

I lost my own dad in 1998, and my father-in-law stepped up and became a father to me, fulfilling his promise.

It was such an honor for me to care for Mr. Radcliff in our home during the last six weeks of his life. As he grew weaker from metastatic lung cancer, we spent a lot of time together. Every morning I would wait at the side of his bed until he was ready to sit up. Then we did our "dance" where I pulled him to standing and rocked side to side, moving to the wheelchair. Every time I would thank him for the dance, and he would respond, "My pleasure."

There were times during the day when I would check on him, and without fail, he was sitting in his recliner with his Bible opened on his knobby knees. He was a regimented man and always had his regular quiet time, using two different devotionals. But as his time on earth grew shorter, his time in God's Word grew longer. He was prepared to meet his Savior, and left us all quite a legacy.

Shame

Childhood sexual abuse shapes people in ways they wish it wouldn't and may not even realize. One of the most common effects is the feeling of shame. I make the distinction between guilt and shame this way: Guilt results because of what you *do*, while shame results from believing what you do is who you *are* or who you *think you are*. Because we sin, we are all declared guilty. It's a judgment against us. Shame takes that judgment and translates it from "you did a bad thing" to "you are a bad person."

Abused children are often taught that the abuse is their fault or that they caused it in some way. The abuser tells the victim that they couldn't stop themselves because of something the victim did, or that the victim deserved it. The victim then assumes that if they caused it to happen, then they must be evil themselves. Simple reasoning.

While our sin can be forgiven and our guilt taken away by the work of the cross, shame can remain. We don't see ourselves as God see us—pure, holy, and white as snow. We still see ourselves as dirty, bad, somehow complicit in the abuse, and unworthy of such great grace. Our shame keeps us from experiencing the freedom and abundant life that Jesus died for.

We can also fall into the trap of believing we *are* our past or we *are* what happened to us, and so we live in a state of shame. While our past will shape us in some ways, it does not determine who we are. God has made us with a purpose in mind. Yes, the devastating things that enter our lives will influence us, and they are meant to, but they do not define us. If we allow God to work in us, he will take those negative experiences and weave them into the tapestry of our lives. They usually end up being the darker, contrasting threads that give the finished tapestry its unique beauty.

Some of us look at that tapestry and instead of seeing that the dark threads make it unique and beautiful, we believe that they ruin the tapestry, destroying its worth. We see what could have been a beautiful piece of art, but to us it is full of holes and mistakes that make it just plain ugly, certainly not something of worth. But that's not how God sees us. Maybe some of the colors in our life's tapestry are not what we would have picked, but what gives it worth—what makes it valuable—is who made it. I can only think of one Picasso that I think is a beautiful piece of art. But I recognize that his other paintings are valuable because they are Picassos, not because of my feelings for them.

The creator of our lives had a special design in mind for us. And because it is *his* design, it is perfect, beautiful, and valuable. It is said that something is worth what someone will pay for it. Jesus gave his life for us, making our worth immeasurable.

Shame also comes from the reaction of our own bodies when we're touched in a sexual way. The abuse I suffered was not violent, and it was perpetrated by someone I knew and liked. I confused the physiological reaction I had when he touched me with an emotional connection. Knowing that what he was doing was wrong but reacting positively to it, I had thought I must want it to happen. Why would my body react to his touch if I didn't want it to? And if that happens when you're a Christian, it can cause you to even doubt your salvation.

Christians know right from wrong. They know sin. They feel the conviction of the Holy Spirit when they sin. Therein lies the confusion and condemnation. They know what is happening is sin, but when their body responds to it, they wonder if they are participating in or even enjoying sin—and if they are, then how can they be saved? Often, those feelings are encouraged by the abuser as part of his or her manipulation.

I didn't understand then that God has made our bodies to react to certain stimuli in certain ways. It wasn't until I learned that as a mature adult that I found real freedom from my abuse and could say with confidence that none of it was my fault. It took close to twenty-five years for me to come to that point. That is why I wrote this book—maybe it will help someone else get there sooner.

Shame is not unique to abuse victims. Even Jesus experienced shame, at the end of his earthly life. Hebrews 12:2 tells us that for the joy set before him (our salvation), Jesus endured the cross, despising the shame. It was shameful to hang on a cross. It was a public display of who you were—a criminal of the worst sort. Jesus was perfectly innocent on that cross. The shame he was bearing was our sin. He became sin for us.

Second Corinthians 5:21 says that he who knew no sin became sin for us, so that we might become the righteousness of God. We can't be righteous or clean or holy on our own. Jesus exchanges our guilt and shame for his righteousness. That is the work of the cross. Because of that work, we *are* righteous. We are holy because He is holy, and that frees us from our sin and shame.

When God looks at us, He no longer sees our sin but Christ's righteousness. Can you say with assurance that you believe God sees you as righteous, that Jesus blood has washed you whiter than snow (Psalm 51:7)?

CHAPTER 11:

Freedom from Bitterness

Going Public

Toward the end of that year of waiting for Mr. R's trial to begin, Doug and I were scheduled to share our testimonies in church. We had just taken over leadership of the youth group and had also welcomed a second little boy into our family. The pastor and his wife encouraged me to include my past and what was happening now into my testimony. I had always left that part out, but they felt it was important to share, so I did.

I shared the circumstances that led to my salvation and some of the struggles God had brought me through. As I turned the page to the last paragraph of my notes, my face heated and my stomach seemed to take up residence in my throat.

Fighting to get the words out without making squeaking sounds as my throat pushed my stomach back into place, I said that there was something I had left out: for most of my childhood, I had been molested, and the man who had done it was currently on trial in another case and I might have to testify. I also shared that I was trusting God to use what I had learned to help others. Closing my notes,

I looked up at the stunned faces, some as flushed as my own, and urged my shaky legs back to my seat.

My dear husband took my hand and whispered that I should be a professional speaker. *Ha!* I thought. *This is a once and done thing, and my insides couldn't take it anyway.*

After the service, several people approached me. A young woman said, "The same thing happened to me with a babysitter. I thought I was the only one." Others said they could hardly believe it because I seemed to have such a perfect life. A police officer from our congregation said, "Thank you for sharing what you did. It is so needed. You have no idea how many lives this affects." Still others treated me like I had the plague.

I had thought some people would have a negative response, but that still took me by surprise, especially because of who they were— pillars of the church. They just didn't want that kind of ugliness to be talked about in church. But it is that kind of thinking that keeps abused Christians from finding complete freedom from their past and their shame. It would take many years for me to understand that. At that time, it just hurt.

Shortly after I shared the story of my abuse for the first time in a public setting, I learned that I would not have to testify in court. My statement was entered into the court record, and they didn't need me to come to court in person. What a relief!

The trial was over quickly, and the monster was sentenced to two to twenty-four months in jail. It was his "first" offense, so he and his lawyer had not expected any jail time, but the judge had taken into consideration the statements given by me and the other woman, which documented a long history of abuse. Mr. R and his lawyer were shocked to hear the judge's decision. He was so sure that he wouldn't spend even a single day in jail. As it turned out, he only served two months.

I admit I was angry that he didn't serve more time. How many women would struggle for the rest of their lives because of his actions, and yet he would only suffer for two months? But again, just like my past, I gave it to God and left it with him. I did my part, and couldn't let bitterness or resentment take root. His punishment was not for me to decide. I was just glad this chapter of my life was closed.

Or was it?

Hero Pastor

As all of this was coming out, my pastor was right there with me. Besides my husband and a few friends, no one has been on my side like he was. He and his wife had counseled many abuse victims—all kinds of abuse. One day he asked me (as many others had) how I could be as together as I was without having had professional counseling. I answered him the same way I answered that question every time: "I understood that when I was saved, Jesus took away not only my sin but also my past. I was a new creation. 'For I have died, and my life was hidden with Christ in God'" (Colossians 3:3).

Amazed, he encouraged me to share my story, saying it would help so many victims. The fact that he was even speaking to me about sexual abuse was profound. During this time, the church was, for the most part, completely silent on these matters. This pastor was an older, self-proclaimed "dumb Dutchman." While he certainly wasn't dumb, he was as Pennsylvania Dutch as they come—and stoic Pennsylvania Dutchmen didn't talk about such things. But not this one. He talked with me about it and encouraged me to minister to others.

He was also an encourager. He challenged those not walking rightly with God, and he mourned with, rejoiced with, taught, and truly pastored his flock. A true hero, he died just a few years ago and will always hold a special place in my heart. I doubt that I would have ministered as I have to other victims, without his encouragement.

Anger, Resentment, Bitterness, Forgiveness

Of course, there were times when I felt anger, sometimes overwhelming anger. It can be easily justified. After all, the Bible talks about righteous anger—being angry but not sinning. That is a part of our everyday lives. When we see a news report about a child who was abused or killed or the abortion rate increasing or evil seeming to prevail in some way, it makes us angry. And it should. But it is a very small step to go from righteous anger to sinful anger. We need to be cautious not to cross the line.

Harboring anger causes resentment. *Resentment* is an accounting term that means to keep an account of or record of. In other words, someone hurts us and we add it to the list of things they've done wrong. When we think of all the things on the list, our resentment turns to bitterness. Nothing that person does or says will be okay because we have allowed bitterness to take root in our heart. A bitter heart will destroy us and could easily be the reason an abuse victim can't move on with their life.

True freedom from anger, resentment, and bitterness does not come without forgiveness. Circumstances may keep you from offering forgiveness to your abuser. Perhaps your abuser is not seeking forgiveness or is no longer living. Still, your heart must be ready to forgive. Remember, you are not forgiving his sin (only God can do that). You are choosing not to hold it against them (not keeping an account).

If you don't have the opportunity to offer forgiveness to your abuser, tell God that you forgive them. He will do a work in your heart that will free you from any anger, resentment, or bitterness that has formed there. When the Enemy brings things to mind that cause anger to well up, you may need to remind yourself that you have forgiven your abuser. Don't give the Enemy any foothold at all in this area.

Besides with the abuser, there may be other times you need to refrain from getting angry and harboring resentments because of your abuse. In my story, the rejection I experienced from friends and church members caused anger. I could feel the resentment starting to take hold. How could Christians treat me badly when I was the victim? I had to remember that my story may make others uncomfortable, or it may bring up bad memories in others that they haven't worked through. It's my responsibility to have a forgiving heart and mind.

I also had the issue of forgiving my mom. Although I had told her about the abuse, she chose to look the other way. Maybe she just didn't want to deal with it as a single mother who was trying to raise her daughters as best she could. It might have been too much for her to handle. Or maybe she really didn't believe he was dangerous.

Whatever the reason, we didn't talk about it between the time I first told her (when I was thirteen) and ten years later when he was arrested. I stopped at her office the day I met with the police to let her know that I was meeting with them, and she fell apart, crying uncontrollably. "You told me. You told me," she kept saying. She had enormous guilt, and through her tears, she asked me to forgive her. I was happy to relieve that burden from her by offering forgiveness.

There is nothing quite like the peace that comes through forgiveness. If you have the opportunity to offer forgiveness to your abuser, what a gift for both of you. The Bible says we have been given the ministry of reconciliation (2 Corinthians 5:11–21). Even though my mom and I had not been estranged, our relationship changed after this. We seemed to love and respect each other in a deeper way, and there were no barriers between us. Any hurt caused by either of us was forgotten.

We are fortunate that God keeps no record of our wrongs. If he did, who could stand? When we sin and ask forgiveness, he hits the *delete* key in our Excel file. It's as if the sin never existed at all. He forgets our sin—or remembers it no more, according to Hebrews 8:12.

Forget is also an accounting term—for example, forgetting a debt or wiping it from the record. That column on the Excel sheet disappears, and he doesn't hit *undo* the next time we sin to check how many times that sin has been committed. It's gone forever. All of our sins—past, present, and future—were nailed to the cross with Jesus. "If we confess our sins, he is faithful and just to forgive us our sins and cleanse us from all unrighteousness" (1 John 1:9).

In a familiar verse like this one, we can cruise right through the terms *faithful and just* without giving much thought to them. *Faithful* makes sense to us. We know that God keeps his promises. But what about *just*? Why is God just to forgive us our sins? The answer again is the cross. Jesus took our punishment for sin when he died on the cross. So justice has been served; Jesus paid what we owe. Therefore, God is just in forgiving our sins because the payment for them has already been made. Jesus stamped our debt *paid in full*, and God the Father accepted that payment.

On an intellectual level, we cannot forget the abuse we have suffered. But we can expunge it from our hearts. Just as we can choose to hold a grudge, we can choose to let it go. Someone once asked Clara Barton, the founder of the American Red Cross, if she remembered a particularly evil deed someone did to her. Her response was, "No; I distinctly remember forgetting that." [4]

When we choose to keep the past in the past, it can't control our present or future. True freedom to live an abundant life can be found in forgiving from our hearts and setting our minds to "forget" our past hurts.

A study of Colossians 3 can truly help you understand who you are in Christ. It's all about putting off the old self (things like anger, resentment, and bitterness) and then putting on the new self (compassion, kindness, and, most of all, love). It says to let the Word of God dwell in you richly. Start there. God's Word can't dwell in you if you don't know it.

So start by reading and studying God's Word. Don't study just the verses or passages that pertain to suffering or abuse or other issues in your life. Study the whole thing. Come up with a plan or try a ready-made reading plan. Study the things you want to reflect in your life—holiness, joy, praise, compassion, kindness, and love.

My favorite Bible chapter is 2 Peter 1. It's a good place to start when studying how to live the Christian life. Verse 3 begins, "His divine power has granted to us all things that pertain to life and godliness." That same power—his divine power—is in us through his Holy Spirit.

Verse 4 says he has granted to us his precious and very great promises; verses 5 to 7 say we should make every effort to supplement our faith with virtue, knowledge, self-control, steadfastness, godliness, brotherly affection, and love; and verse 8 wraps it up by saying that when these things are ours and are increasing, they keep us from being ineffective and unfruitful. Isn't that the opposite of what holding a grudge does (makes us ineffective and unfruitful)? I encourage you to read the chapter in its entirety and take in its benefits.

When you are actively working toward these things and trusting the Holy Spirit to work in you, your life will continually reflect these positive qualities, resulting in unshakable joy with no room for anger, resentment, and bitterness.

CHAPTER 12:

Broken but Free

I had hoped that the completion of the trial and the sentencing of Mr. R would finally close the lid on the box that held this phase of my life. I was content to stuff it in a closet, way back on a dark shelf, never to be reopened. But sharing it in my testimony popped off a corner of that lid until the contents of the box spilled out into the light for everyone to see. Even though I never wanted sexual abuse to be the thing in my life that God would use to help others, it was.

So I embraced the opportunities God brought to share how I found healing and freedom in him. In our ministry to teens, the Lord brought hurting girls my way so I could comfort with the comfort I had received from him. I was asked to share my story with groups outside our church family. The more I talked about it, the more I saw that there were other victims who needed to find freedom from their pasts but didn't know how. There was joy in helping others find freedom in Christ—true freedom with no condemnation, Romans 8 kind of freedom.

After speaking at one women's retreat, I was amazed by how many women came to me afterward to express how much they were affected by my testimony. One woman especially stuck out. She was a sweet, gentle soul in her seventies. She had been molested as a young girl and had carried the shame of it all those years. That day she realized she was not responsible for someone else's sin.

The theme of that retreat was "Standing Stones," marking the times that God had done something of significance in our walk with him. That retreat would be one of the standing stones in her life, a time she could look back on when she finally found freedom from her past.

For some victims, like the woman at the retreat, freedom comes with just a word aptly spoken. For others, the struggle takes longer and issues need to be worked through. But the remedy is the same. True freedom is found in Christ, no matter how big or small the chains that bind you.

Some people are abused one time and it affects them for the rest of their lives. Others have no ill effects from abusive encounters. We should be careful not to condemn those whose experience is different from our own. False guilt can be projected onto someone who was abused but doesn't show any scars from it. It could be that they really don't have any. Praise God and leave them alone.

On the opposite side of that are those who can't get past the abuse of their childhood. It is possible to be completely free from the past. I can say that because God promises it. He is the only one who can make us new and cause the old to pass away. But to think that it cannot be done, limits God. It limits his love, his mercy, his grace, and his power, all of which are yours through the Holy Spirit.

Blame

Perhaps you blame God for the abuse you suffered. After all, he could have stopped it from happening or intervened at any time, but he didn't. Maybe you can't move on in your Christian walk because you don't trust the One you are walking with.

In Lamentations 3, Jeremiah says that God has "driven … me into darkness" (v. 2). He is the one who "has broken my bones" (v. 4) and "made my chains heavy" (v. 7). He "made [me] the laughing stock" (v. 14) and "filled me with bitterness" (v. 15). The Lord is "a bear lying in wait for me" (v. 10), and he "turned aside my steps and tore me to pieces" (v. 11). Yes, he did say these things about God. But in the context of Lamentations, he is describing God's wrath against Israel because of their disobedience; this is his judgment and wrath poured out on them.

Later in that same chapter, God shows his great mercy to Israel—mercies that "are new every morning" (v. 23). It says that God is "good to those who wait for Him" (v. 25) and "For the Lord will not cast off forever, though he causes grief, he will have compassion according to His steadfast love" (vv. 31–32). We are exhorted to "examine our ways and return to the LORD" (v. 40). In his holiness, God cannot let disobedience go unpunished. Fortunately for us, Jesus has taken our punishment on himself on the cross.

It is not God who causes sinful things to happen to us. And while he could intervene—and often does—we can trust that there is purpose in our suffering. Don't believe Satan's lie that the abuse you suffered was God's fault. If anyone is at fault for sin, it is Satan, the father of lies. Remember, he wants to destroy you and keep you from the life God has for you.

Whether you believe that God *ordains* suffering or *allows* suffering, we can agree that he could stop it or intervene in some way. Are you angry with God for the suffering you have endured? Do you blame him for all the things you've had to deal with because of abuse? Talk to him about it. One of the blessings of suffering is that it drives us to God, usually on our knees.

Sometimes it is expressed in anger, shaking a fist at God or wondering where he was. We can take our anger, doubt, and questions to him because he is our heavenly Father who loves us. He won't turn away because we are angry or confused. He will listen and comfort us—and sometimes, not always, he will show us the purpose for our suffering.

I hope that by introducing you to some of the heroes in my life, I have helped you think about who God put in your life to rescue you. You're alive and reading this book, so clearly God kept you from being completely lost to the darkness. Look back and identify the people or circumstances he used to "keep" you. They are there, and it may help you in your journey to freedom to see them, as well as God's love and compassion by providing them.

Some victims will have no problem accepting this information and moving on all by themselves. But if you need professional help, seek it out. A Christian counselor or pastor can be very helpful in walking you through the steps of overcoming your past.

Hero Sons

The hardest conversations I've had in relating my story of childhood sexual abuse came when I needed to tell my three sons. The first one was the hardest. Doug and I were working with the youth group at church, and our oldest son was about to enter it. Because the subject came up quite often with the teens, Doug and I decided it was time to share the story with our own seventh grader.

My oldest son and I walked around our little town just chatting, and then I got around to what I really wanted to talk to him about.

I wasn't going to give him any details, but I still had to force the words from my mouth: "For many years during my childhood, I was molested." There, it was out. We talked about it a little bit more.

Why was this so hard? I'd talked to hundreds of people in large groups. But that night, walking with my son on our familiar streets, there was a knife turning in my heart with every word. I guess because as his mom, I never wanted any of the horrible stuff of life to touch him. Now it had.

One by one, as each son reached seventh grade, I repeated the same story on the same walk. Each one was slightly easier than the first, but not by much. My oldest says he remembers exactly where he was—the street name and the very place on the sidewalk—when he first learned about my abusive past. Now that they are grown, my boys remind me often how proud they are that I didn't stay silent. They are the lights of my life, blessings of God's glorious grace.

Brokenness

The word I hear over and over when talking with victims of childhood sexual abuse is *broken*. They feel like they're not whole; they are broken in so many ways.

This is not such a bad thing. God uses broken people. Without brokenness, people become puffed up and full of pride, and often see no need to submit to God. Psalm 34:18 says, "The Lord is near to the brokenhearted and saves the crushed in spirit." Is that you? Have you felt brokenhearted and crushed in spirit? That's okay. The Lord is near to you, and he can use you because of your brokenness. You will be able to reveal God's glory in ways others cannot.

Second Corinthians 4:6–9 tells us, "For God who said, 'Let light shine out of darkness,' has shone in our hearts to give the light of the knowledge of the glory of God in the face of Jesus Christ. But we have this treasure in jars of clay, to show the surpassing power belongs to God and not to us. We are afflicted but not crushed; perplexed but not driven to despair, persecuted but not forsaken, struck down but not destroyed."

This passage teaches us that we are jars of clay, easily broken, displaying God's power and glory in our weakness. We can only show God's glory when we are broken. It is then that his glory is revealed as it spills out of our broken places. And God's grace extends more and more as we rely on him. Give him your brokenness and trust Him to use it for his glory.

Despair

What if your brokenness has already led to despair? You just don't see any way out of your circumstances, and you can't live in them any longer. Perhaps, like me, you told a parent or other adult about your abuse, but they did nothing. You feel you are at a dead end and this life is too much for you to handle.

Suicide. It starts as a thought: *There is a way out.* Then it grows into a plan: *If I take this bottle of pills …,* or *I know where Dad keeps his gun,* or *I could crash my car into a wall; that way it will look like an accident.*

The car crash was my plan. Right after the abuse ended, my mom and I had a huge fight, and I felt like life was not worth the pain and effort. I was in despair and wanted it to end. At the time, I didn't know the abuse was really over. Difficult things were piling up, and I didn't think I could take anymore.

That morning when I left the house, I had every intention of crashing. I thought about where to crash. A friend had died in a car accident when her car went off a local bridge, and I considered that option. Large trees and buildings also might work. I didn't want to do anything that might injure someone else. Then the thought entered my mind that I might not die. I might just be severely injured, possibly permanently. That thought ended my plan but not my despair. I believe it was God who brought the thought of serious injury instead of death to my mind.

I am so thankful to God that he kept me from following through on that plan. His plan was much better and saved my life for eternity. Abuse victims can be gripped by despair when they feel utterly alone in their suffering with no way of escape. They tried to get out on their own, or maybe they sought help, but their circumstances haven't changed. Satan is whispering in their ear, "There is a way out. Just end it. Your life isn't worth living." Remember, Satan comes to kill and destroy. That's his goal in all of life. He doesn't want any of us to have life, and certainly not abundant life that shines forth God's glory.

Don't give in to despair. Don't give in to Satan. God has so much planned for your life. Plans that include life, hope, joy, and peace. Trust him. Keep telling someone until you find a person who will listen and act. You might have to bypass your family and go to the police. That's the right thing to do.

Too often, when abuse occurs within a family, the family wants to keep it private. They want to deal with it on their own, but you need real help. A family who thinks they can handle it without getting the proper authorities involved is in denial. You won't receive the help and security you need without telling someone who has the authority and ability to force change. That person may be a police officer, or maybe a teacher, youth leader, coach, pastor, or guidance counselor. Anyone who works with minors is obligated by law to report abuse to the police.

Abuse victims often don't want to cause trouble within their family. They don't want to be hated by family members and worry that they will lose the rest of their family. The truth is, they might. I have seen families take the side of the abuser. It's difficult for people to believe that a loved one could do such horrible things. They consider the victim a troublemaker, the one who broke up their family. But it is the abuser who is the troublemaker, not the victim.

It is time light conquers darkness. Darkness in this case is silence. Someone in the family must step up and shine light in that darkness. Even if you lose your family, you will find life, and there will be others who will become family to you. Be strong and courageous. It won't be easy, but in the end, doing the right thing will be the beginning of finding freedom.

Freedom

So what does it mean to be free from the past? What is freedom in Christ?

It doesn't mean we pretend the past never happened. On the contrary, God will use the hard things from our past to help others and cause us to grow closer to him. But we don't want to live there. It's not our destination, just a stop along the road. He has so much for us in the present and has prepared a grand future for us.

Being free of my past means it doesn't control me. It doesn't control my mind, my emotions, my outlook, or any other part of my life. Paul said in Philippians 3:13–14 that Christ has made him his own and in order to become more like Christ, "forgetting what lies behind and straining forward to what lies ahead, I press on toward the goal for the prize of the upward call of God in Christ Jesus." He doesn't stay in one place; he moves forward, even straining to get there.

Because we are in Christ, we are completely free. He has set us free. It wasn't something that we did. It wasn't that we got off on a technicality but deep down we know someday the other shoe will drop and everyone will know we aren't really free. No, Jesus purchased our freedom with his own blood. And because he was the one who set us free, we are free indeed. Freedom in Christ is complete. It is final. It can never be taken away.

Freedom brings rest—rest from the torment of abuse and rest from despair. Your mind can turn off. You don't need to be constantly thinking about your circumstances and ways out. You can live and even sleep in peace. Isaiah 26:3 reminds us that God keeps us in perfect peace when our mind is stayed on him.

Freedom means living an abundant life—a life full of joy, peace, love, new experiences and challenges, adventure, and you name it. You can do it because you are no longer chained to your past.

CHAPTER 13:

Getting a Grip

Triggers

I mentioned triggers earlier. For abuse victims, triggers can be everywhere—a face in a crowd, a smell, a memory, a song, a place. The list goes on and on. For me, it was the smell of a certain cologne.

When my husband and I first married, we moved away from where we grew up and looked for a new church home. When we first visited the church we would eventually call home, I always sat right at the aisle because of my claustrophobia. But the first time we had communion there, my aisle seat nearly became a catapult.

Unbeknownst to me, the elders of this church served communion by leaning into the pew and holding the tray for each person to receive the bread and then did that again with the cup. The elder who served our pew leaned over top of me to reach the people sitting in the middle of the row and happened to be wearing the same cologne as the man who abused me.

In a moment's time, I was right back on his patio and the flight response was trying to take over. If pews came with an ejection button, I would have hit it! You can picture the bread flying through the sanctuary and everyone gaping at the crazy woman bolting down the aisle. Somehow, I managed to remain in my seat. My husband recognized the look of panic on my face and gently but firmly put his hand on my leg, keeping me grounded for the moment. Since then, I've always sat in the middle of the pew, where I am safe from leaners.

I was also very uncomfortable with seeing dads put an arm around their preteen daughters. I had to talk myself off the ledge more than once, telling myself that this was perfectly normal behavior for a loving father. I don't know why this even bothered me, since I never had abuse issues with my dad. In fact, I had never felt safer and more secure than when I was cuddled on the couch with him. But it did. There were also times before my abuse became public knowledge that I had to leave the room if a speaker started talking about sexual abuse. I just couldn't stay in my seat. Sometimes the triggers are known and sometimes they aren't. Learning how to deal with them is the key. And that key, once again, is the truth of Scripture.

You probably know what the triggers are for you. And you might find more as life goes on. You can set yourself up for failure by putting yourself in situations that will trigger a memory. If you're not at a place in your journey where you can handle that, then don't go there. Down the road, along another part of the journey, you may get there. Don't feel guilty if you simply can't participate in something. Healing is more important than saving face.

In a recent report on the arrest of college coach Jerry Sandusky's son, Jeffrey, for similar sexual abuse crimes, the reporter wrote, "For victims of child abuse, even those who never encountered Sandusky or barely even heard of him, the emergence of another high-profile case will cause them to revisit haunting memories."[5] I remember when the Jerry Sandusky scandal broke. As I listened to the stories coming out, my tears flowed unchecked. I imagined those innocent children and the horror they endured by someone they trusted and looked up to.

Another coach saw Sandusky and a boy in the shower, made eye contact, and walked away. That scene haunted me. It played out in my mind. I could see the boy's face, pleading for the man to do something, to stop it. And I felt his despair when that man walked away. I imagined the words Sandusky said to that boy as the other coach left the room: "See, it's no big deal. People know and they don't care." Then I imagined that child being overwhelmed with the realization that this was now his life—that this man was telling him the truth. It took me right back to memories of my own abuse, and it was hard to listen. It took a mountain of prayer to control my anger and keep bitterness at bay.

When I listen to someone else's story now, I still feel uncomfortable and memories do come back, but they don't control me. I've learned that memories are just that—something that took place in the past. They don't need to affect my life today, and I don't dwell on the memory. It takes its proper place as part of my past while I turn my focus to the person talking and their story and how I can empathize with or even minister to them.

Sometimes triggers can be helpful. If someone in your life gives you the willies, don't just reject those feelings. Abuse victims tend to be perceptive about when something isn't right with someone. Be wise. Sometimes those feelings are simply an overreaction to a trigger, but I have learned to trust my instincts with people. Those who haven't been abused often overlook a person's inappropriate behavior, but someone who has been abused will pick up on things that are off much more quickly. Share your feelings with someone you trust.

Restoration

As a young Christian, I read the Bible voraciously. That kind of interest led me to study the minor prophets. While I didn't know what most of them were trying to say and knew nothing of commentaries, I still found gems in those books. In the book of Joel, I grabbed onto God's promise of restoration.

Joel is an account of God's judgment on Israel through destruction of their land by four different types of locusts. So complete was the devastation that God said, "Has such a thing ever happened in your day or in the days of your fathers? Tell your children of it, and let your children tell their children, and their children to another generation" (Joel 2:3). The scope of this destructive judgment was like nothing else they had ever experienced.

God called Israel to repent: "'Yet even now,' declares the LORD, 'return to me with all your heart, with fasting, with weeping, and with mourning; and rend your hearts and not your garments.' Return to the LORD YOUR GOD, for he is gracious and merciful, slow to anger, and abounding in steadfast love" (Joel 2:12–13).

"Rend your hearts and not your garments" refers to the practice of tearing one's clothes to show sorrow or repentance. God didn't want simply an outward demonstration of repentance; he wanted their hearts in true repentance. And then because he abounds in love, God brought about restoration. In this same chapter God describes himself as a jealous God. He wants us, and he is jealous of anything that takes our affections away from him. It is a beautiful picture of his character. While we do nothing to deserve them, he continually lavishes love and mercy upon us.

When the people turned to the Lord, he fulfilled his promises of restoration. The land yielded fruit, the vine gave its full yield, the threshing floors were full of grain, and the vats overflowed with oil. Everything was restored to overflowing.

Joel 2:25–27 are most precious to me: "I will restore to you the years that the swarming locust has eaten, the hopper, the destroyer, and the cutter, my great army, which I sent among you. You shall eat in plenty and be satisfied, and praise the name of the LORD your God, who has dealt wondrously with you. And my people shall never again be put to shame. You shall know that I am in the midst of Israel, and that I am the LORD your God, and there is none else. And my people shall never again be put to shame."

Joel 2 has had special meaning to me as I worked through the issues of childhood sexual abuse. Judgment is described as destroying locusts, four different kinds, so utterly destructive that whatever the first locust left, the second locust destroyed, and so on with the third and fourth, so that Israel was completely destroyed. I personalize the passage in this way: The first locust in my life was the abuse, the second was fear, the third was despair, and the fourth was shame. It didn't escape my notice that God calls the locusts "his" army, which "he" sent. In Israel's case, the locusts were his judgment. In my case, they were the things he would allow so that I could know and serve him better.

Being a Christian is not an easy road. For growth to happen, pruning must be done. There is discipline, which is never pleasant at the moment. Even so, we can trust the One who does the pruning and disciplining because he is perfect and loves us completely. Even though God brought the destruction, he also wants to restore what was lost. I can attest to that in my own life.

God has more than restored the years the locusts have stolen from me. But even if he hadn't done that, in view of eternity, my suffering on this earth is truly not worth comparing with the glory that is to be revealed to us (Romans 8:18). But God still seems to want to restore the years we have lost here in this lifetime. It is grace upon grace.

Some may not see promises fulfilled in their lifetime, but often God does give a special gift of restoration: "And after you have suffered a little while, the God of all grace, who has called you to his eternal glory in Christ, will himself restore, confirm, strengthen, and establish you" (1 Peter 5:10). In no way does God owe us restored lives. But his compassion is so great that he does restore us.

God cares about our pain and sorrow and suffering. Psalm 56:8–9 tells us, "You have kept count of my tossings and put my tears in your bottle; are they not in your book? Then my enemies will turn back in the day when I call. This I know, that God is for me." While he hasn't kept a record of our sin, God has kept a record of our tears. He has marked them all down and knows every one that is shed. When he comes to reign as King, "'he will wipe away every tear from their eyes, and death shall be no more, neither shall there be mourning, nor crying, nor pain, for the former things have passed away'" (Revelation 21:4).

And just as God promises to wipe away our tears and restore us and make up for all the pain we endured, he also promises to punish those who caused our pain: "But as for the cowardly, the faithless, the detestable, as for murderers, the sexually immoral, the sorcerers, idolaters, and all liars, their portion will be in the lake which burns with fire and sulfur, which is the second death" (Revelation 21:8).

The Bible is clear that those who are enemies of God's people will suffer his wrath. We don't need to seek revenge. Perhaps in this life, your abuser will be prosecuted, but perhaps not. Maybe, as far as we can tell, they will not suffer at all in this life. That is not ours to decide. But eventually, they will answer for their sin.

CHAPTER 14

In the Grip of Grace

" Therefore, since we have been justified by faith, we have peace with God through our Lord Jesus Christ. Through him we have also obtained access by faith into this **grace** in which we stand, and we rejoice in hope of the glory of God. Not only that, but we rejoice in our sufferings, knowing that suffering produces endurance, and endurance produces character, and character produces hope, and hope does not put us to shame, because God's love has been poured into our hearts through the Holy Spirit who has been given to us" (Romans 5:1–5, emphasis mine).

Grace. What is it? You may know the theological answer, that it is God's unmerited favor, or receiving what we don't deserve. That's true. We cannot earn God's grace, and we don't deserve it. He freely and gladly bestows it on us, not now and then but to live in always.

So what does it mean to stand in grace? Well, without God's grace, we could never stand at all. Think for a moment about what God saved you from. Some will say he has saved them from hell. Others will say that he saved them from sin. True, but what he really saved us from was himself. He saved us from his own wrath—a wrath in which no one can stand.

Revelation 6:16–17 says, "Calling to the mountains and the rocks, 'Fall on us and hide us from the face of him who is seated on the throne, and from the wrath of the Lamb, for the great day of their wrath has come, and who can stand?'" Except for God's grace, no one would stand in the judgment. But because he desires to lavish his love and grace on his chosen people, he saves us from his wrath by pouring it out on his own son in our place: "In him we have redemption through his blood, the forgiveness of our trespasses, according to the **riches of his grace, which he lavished upon us**, in all wisdom and insight making known to us the mystery of his will, according to his purpose, which he set forth in Christ" (Ephesians 1:7–9, emphasis mine).

That is God's saving grace, but there is even more to it. His grace is seen in the everyday things of life as well. So often God shows his grace in little ways, like the timing of events, protection in a dangerous situation, or having the right words to say to someone in a time of need. His grace is worked out in so many ways that make our lives more abundant.

I tell people that I am God's favorite. Once they get over the shock at such a statement (and back away from the coming lightning bolt), I explain what I mean. Of course, God doesn't have favorites, but he makes me feel like I must be his favorite by the things he does for me and the way he shows his grace to me each day. Then I tell them the story of how I learned that I am, indeed, his favorite.

We were on vacation at our Maine camp. It was a beautiful, sunny August morning, and we spent the morning swimming and playing in the lake. One of our favorite games is King of the Rock. About fifty feet from our dock is a huge rock that pokes out of the water about a foot. It has a ledge on one side, where you can stand with your head out of the water. The other side slopes gently, and the back side drops off sharply to where the depth of the lake is about eight feet. It's perfectly suited for our game. Doug, our two oldest boys, and I would scramble up onto the rock and try to knock each other off the deep-end side.

On this day, we had been playing for a long time. Worn out and ready for lunch, we swam back to the dock. Doug offered to make lunch and bring it out to us, so the boys ran off on another adventure and I wrapped up in my towel and sat down on the dock.

The sun felt so good on my back. As I relaxed in its warmth, I swung my feet with my toes just barely touching the water. Several curious sunfish circled around them, deciding if they were food or something more sinister. While watching the sunnies, I noticed something sparkly on the bottom of the lake. It glistened in the sun, and my first thought was that it was one of Bob's beer tabs that have been emerging from the lake bottom for a decade.

Will they never end? I thought. But then I realized, *It's not shiny like the aluminum tabs. It's sparkles more like a diamond.* Reflexively, I glanced at the ring finger of my left hand. Where the diamond of my engagement ring had been, I was greeted by gaping prongs. The diamond was gone!

Just as panic was about to take over, I looked in the water again. *Sparkles more like a diamond. It couldn't be, could it?* We had been swimming and playing all over the lake. What were the chances that my diamond could be right here, in only two feet of water, right at my feet?

Dropping my towel on the dock, I gently eased myself into the water. But at that angle, nothing sparkled. I called for my oldest son, who at the time was around ten years old. "Bring your goggles," I said. "I need you to get something out of the water."

He stepped into the water, and I guided him to the sparkling. He reached for the bottom, covered with rocks and sand, and pulled out a petite but very sparkly diamond. When he handed it to me, I kissed him and told him he was my hero (it started young).

In our cabin, I grabbed a tissue, then wrapped up the diamond and sealed it in an envelope, along with the ring of prongs, to be repaired back home. I relayed the entire drama to Doug, again asking (this time aloud), "What are the chances of that diamond being lost right by the dock, and me sitting in just the right position to see it?" He replied, "The only answer is you must be God's favorite."

Yes, that's it. I am God's favorite. Obviously, I had found some special favor from God for him to show this kindness to me. That special favor is his grace. And, no, it isn't just for me. But when I recognize it in my life, it makes feel like I really am his favorite. So I remind my friends and family on a regular basis that I am God's favorite.

It is his grace that chooses us and calls us (Galatians 1:15), his grace that saves us (Ephesians 2:8), his grace that justifies us (Romans 3:24), and his grace that keeps us. We simply are nothing without his grace. It is also his grace that delivers us from suffering. God doesn't want his children to suffer, but because of sin and the purposes we discussed earlier, it is necessary. But my time of suffering was cut off because of God's grace.

In listening to news reports of natural disasters, I've noticed that certain media outlets try to twist the devastation and loss of life into a reckoning of God's grace. They fire questions at well-known Christian leaders: "How could a God of love allow this to happen?" or "Is God all-powerful or all-loving? Certainly he cannot be both to allow this."

What they don't understand is that because of God's grace and his love, the disaster was limited. There are always stories of lives and homes that were spared. We have never lived in a world where God is not present, holding all things together. Even in the worst disasters or circumstances, God is holding back evil. He does allow what is in his will, and I am sure he uses natural disasters within that context. But it all could be so much worse.

The earth is under the curse too. It is dying, so weather and disasters will continue and will probably get worse. But that is within God's control and his grace. And let's not be a Pollyanna about God's grace. It is endless and knows no limits for those who love God, "but grace was given to each one of us according to the measure of Christ's gift" (Ephesians 4:7). The "measure of Christ's gift" is beyond our comprehension. Even so, for those who are his enemies, a time will come when his grace will be cut off—removed from this world— and none will be spared from his wrath.

Those of us who know God and have experienced his grace need to be ambassadors of his grace. We extend grace to others when our speech builds up (Ephesians 4:29), when we offer comfort and hope (2 Thessalonians 3:10), and when we use our gifts to bless others (1 Peter 4:10). Even in our weakness, God's grace is sufficient. It is when we are weak that God's grace shines brightest as his power becomes evident. Our power to overcome sin is God's grace. John Piper puts it this way: "Grace is not simply leniency when we have sinned. Grace is the enabling gift of God not to sin. Grace is power, not just pardon." [6]

It is his grace at work in you that will allow you to conquer all the baggage that comes with abuse as well as share your story to help others. "For it is all for your sake, so that as grace extends to more and more people it may increase thanksgiving, to the glory of God"

(2 Corinthians 4:15). Bringing glory to God is our ultimate goal in life. It is his grace that allows us to take the terrible and make it glorious. Seventeenth-century pastor Christopher Love said, "Grace is but glory begun, and glory is but grace perfected."[7]

It would seem unfinished if we were to end this chapter without mentioning mercy. God's saving grace is because of his mercy: "But God, being rich in mercy, because of the great love with which he loved us, even when we were dead in our trespasses, made us alive together with him—by grace you have been saved" (Ephesians 2:4–5). The two work in tandem. "Let us then with confidence draw near to the throne of grace, that we may receive mercy and find grace to help in time of need" (Hebrews 4:16).

God's grace is receiving what we don't deserve. His mercy is *not* receiving what we do deserve. We deserve eternal punishment in hell, severed from the love, kindness, and grace of God forever. But because of his great mercy, he took what we deserved and laid it on his Son, Jesus. The words of the classic hymn "Amazing Grace" beautifully illustrate God's mercy and grace: "Amazing grace, how sweet the sound, that saved a wretch like me. I once was lost, but now am found, was blind but now I see." Even his saving grace is because of his mercy.

The longer I walk with God, the more wretched my sin is to me and the more amazing his grace and mercy. Praise God for his act of mercy in placing my sin and wretchedness on the cross with Jesus and lavishing his grace upon me. My childhood experiences were not always good, not even okay, but God in his mercy did bring the worst of those experiences to an end and in his grace brought so much good into my life. Then he used those experiences to allow me to show his grace and mercy to other people.

One of the beatitudes is, "Blessed are the merciful, for they will receive mercy" (Matthew 5:7). We glorify God when we show mercy to others, and it makes us happy to do so. When we are offended or hurt in some way, to attack the offender (or at least be happy when something bad happens to them) is a natural reaction. But going against what's natural and extending mercy (overlooking the offense), even though the person doesn't deserve it, will bring you joy.

It doesn't seem like it should, and I can't explain it, except to say that God made it so. As we show mercy, he gives us a tiny glimpse of what he has done for us. I think that is why we get such happiness from extending mercy to others. This might be too hard for you right now as it pertains to your abuser (and I certainly don't want you to put yourself in danger of being abused again), but there may come a time when you have the opportunity to show mercy, and I encourage you to do it. Micah 6:8 sums up the Christian life so well: "What does the LORD require of you? To act justly and to love mercy and to walk humbly with your God" (NIV).

I've talked about God's grace and mercy throughout this book. His grace has been evident to me as I look back at my life, especially in the heroes he brought into it. For a long time, I was in the grip of darkness, thinking that's where I would always be, but God's grace and mercy broke that grip. Now I live in the grip of grace, and that grip can never be broken.

Practical Tips for Parents and the Church

I have found, over the years, that parents and other adults need to be more aware of the people interacting with their children. Pedophiles seek out children, so they go where children are. That means they are trolling playgrounds, hanging around schools, sitting in church pews, swimming at community pools, socializing at homeschool fairs, coaching school and community teams, driving school buses, and stalking the Internet. Wherever children are, they are.

I attended homeschool fairs for years, both as a homeschool mom and then as a vendor. It never ceased to trouble me that so many parents would allow their children to wander a huge venue with no supervision. (And, no, sending a six-year-old to wander around with a ten-year-old is *not* supervision. It's a recipe for disaster.)

As a vendor, I would have kids at my booth all day. Their parents had no idea where they were or what they were doing. Since I was there to recruit homeschooling families to raise Seeing Eye puppies, I had puppies at my booth, and they were wriggling little kid magnets.

These parents and children had never met any of the employees at our booth, and they knew nothing about us except that we brought puppies. While they were fortunate that we were not only harmless but would also watch out for the children around us, I had to wonder if the parents had never heard of pedophiles luring children with puppies. Never assume that other adults within your spectrum are good people who only do what's right. And don't be naïve in thinking that something labeled *Christian* is a completely safe place.

Be responsible for your children, and keep them in view at all times. Don't put the burden of responsibility on your older children. What if something does happen? Now you'll be dealing with two problems: you have a child or children who have been hurt and a child or children who were responsible for them. That would be the case if your child simply fell and was injured. But what if the child is molested? A few moments can affect a child for the rest of their life. And they may not tell you about it. Remember, they will be lied to by the adult abuser. But when the truth comes out, how will the child who was responsible for their care feel? That burden should never be put on a child.

Maybe most disturbing, pedophiles are also relatives and friends. In fact, most victims are abused by a relative, a friend of the family, or someone they knew and trusted prior to the abuse. Probably the most troubling and possibly the most damaging sexual abuse is in the context of parents and pastors. The people the child loves and trusts the most betray them, usually in the guise of a loving relationship. I once heard of a pastor who told a child that when two people love each other, a sexual relationship is natural and blessed by God. It made me sick to my stomach.

Parents need to give their children tools to rightly communicate what's going on in their lives. Even young children need to know the real names of body parts, or at least words which are exactly understood by both parent and child. They should know it is inappropriate to touch others' private areas or to be touched in those areas by others, and be able to communicate any such contact.

We prepare children for so many things. They know that if they are on fire, they should "stop, drop, and roll," but children are much more likely to be sexually abused than to catch on fire. Why not teach them an equally simple montage like, "yell, run, tell"? Just the words alone would cause a child to understand that this situation is wrong and it is okay to cause a scene.

It's time to look past "stranger danger." Since abusers are usually known to the child, teach your child how to find a stranger (instead of being fearful of them) who will most likely help them. Of course, a police officer is a safe choice. Other safe choices would be pretty much any adult in public, especially another parent. Good parents naturally watch out for children, even those who are not their own. When you're out with your child, take a minute to scan the crowd and point out strangers who would be safe and tell your child why they should trust them. Also point out strangers who seem to be poor choices if they need help. Kids should know that if the first person from whom they seek help doesn't do anything, they should go to someone else and keep asking for help until they get it.

I once heard a story about a young boy named Martin who sang with a boys' choir and went on tour with them. This was a Christian group, with chaperones from the church. They would stay in churches along their tour, in makeshift bedrooms created from Sunday School classrooms.

One night one of the chaperones woke Martin and told him to follow him. They went to another room where no one was staying, and there the chaperone told Martin what a good job he was doing in the choir. He hugged the boy, then moved the boy's hand to his crotch. Confused and scared, Martin didn't know what to do. When it was over, he returned to his bed, unsure of what had happened.

Upon returning from the choir tour, Martin tried to tell his mom what had happened, but he lacked the vocabulary. She didn't understand what he was saying, so she brushed it off and told Martin that the chaperone was probably just pleased with his performance. Misunderstanding, miscommunication, lack of proper vocabulary, and dismissing the thought that something bad could happen within the church left Martin with no way to get help or get out of his situation. Even if Martin had only known that it was okay to run away, his situation would have been better.

I've also found that a common misconception of parents is the belief that their child thinks like they do, like an adult. This is not the case. Children think like children. The most mature six-year-old may think like an eight-year-old but not like an adult. They just don't have the life experience—and wisdom that comes with it—to think like adults. I have seen children completely unattended at homeschool fairs, church gatherings, community pools, and other places. Parents have no idea with whom their kids are interacting or what that interaction includes. They assume because these places are "safe," the people in attendance are also safe. Not true.

Children naturally believe that adults are telling them the truth. If they are lied to continually by adults, they will believe it to be reality. So when a child is told that the abuse is their fault, they believe that. When they are told the abuser will hurt them or their family if they tell someone, they believe that. For a child to confide in an adult that they are being abused takes more courage than most adults possess. Believe them.

Some signs to watch for would be a child who is withdrawn, doesn't want to go certain places, becomes angry or destructive, or is unusually interested in their private areas—or any major shift in personality or behavior. Every child is different. While abused children may show similar behaviors, know *your* child and what is unusual in them.

Please be aware that a child may not express any signs of abuse at all. If the abuse started at a very young age, they may think it is normal, especially if they have been groomed to think that way.

I recently spoke to a pastor about children whose father had been arrested for the sexual abuse of his daughters. The pastor's comment was, "The girls are not showing any signs of abuse." That's a dangerous position to take. I'm sure that, during my childhood, my pastor and Sunday School teachers would have said the same thing. Every report card I got in elementary school said, *Doesn't participate in class, Quiet, Keeps to herself.* My teachers assumed that was just my personality—that I was little, quiet, and shy; there was no reason to believe I was being abused. I laughed and played just like the other kids. I had friends, was well-behaved, and never caused trouble. No one knew.

Parents of teens should watch for the same things mentioned above, plus changes in how they dress (more provocatively or adding layers to hide their bodies), friends, and hurting themselves (cutting, alcohol, drugs, etc.). The most important thing all parents can do is cultivate a relationship where their children are free to talk about anything with them. For parents of preteen and teen kids, this means very uncomfortable topics, and you can't freak out. What will you do when your teen or preteen asks you about pornography they have seen? What will you do or say if they tell you they masturbated because of it?

Know that sexual abuse includes showing pornography to a minor. Always ask them where they saw it and who they were with. If you freak out, yell, break down and cry, or ignore them, they will not come to you again. Have a plan, expect it to happen, and know what to say and how to respond in love and acceptance. Believe me, I have answered questions calmly and matter-of-factly and then retreated to my room or car to cry it out and seek God's wisdom.

Don't be afraid to say, "I don't know, but let's find answers to your questions." Parents must keep the lines of communication open. Kids need to know that their parents are safe—they are safe to talk to, they are safe to run to, they are safe to confide in. Parents will end up being the safety line between their child and the authorities and abuser. They are key to allowing the child the freedom to tell their story without fear, and giving them all the support they need.

I know that this information may terrify some parents, which can make them hypervigilant to the point that they see a pedophile in every friendly adult their child encounters. Rest assured that most adults who work with kids do so because they genuinely love children. It's a good thing that children, especially teens and those from single-parent homes, have Christian adults in their lives who model the love of God.

My husband and I have served as volunteers in youth ministry for over thirty-five years. We do it because we have a burden for teens and actually love being around them. Most youth workers, Sunday School teachers, school teachers, and childcare workers feel the same way. Watch for things like an adult giving your child gifts, inviting them to one-on-one outings, or offering to drive them to events. Those are the kinds of things that are warning signs that something is not right.

The church plays a role too. Instead of talking about these things behind closed doors, or not talking about them at all, bring the darkness into the light where it can be overcome. Let us not condemn, ignore, or shame those who have suffered wrong. Rather, let us help, support, and comfort those who have suffered. It is way past time for the church to stop shrinking back from these difficult and uncomfortable topics. If your church needs help to better understand how to assist victims, many seminars, books, and Bible studies are available for church leaders.

Youth workers and Sunday School teachers should be trained in proper interaction with children. Touching children may not be appropriate, or it may be just what the child needs. Workers should also learn the signs of abuse so they can help a struggling child (and be aware that the child may not exhibit unusual behavior because they believe their life is like everyone else's). Standards must be in place, such as never being alone with a child, never driving one child to an event, and never counseling a child of the opposite gender alone. If your state does not require mandatory background checks, do them anyway. These are simple starting points to making the children's ministries a safe place for children, where they can learn of God's love and grow in Him without fear.

Ephesians 4 is a good place for the church to start. It begins by exhorting us to walk in a manner worthy of our calling—in humility, gentleness, patience, and bearing with one another in love. Just working at this one sentence would improve the relationships within the body of Christ. Be humble and consider others more important than yourself.

Put children's needs before your class schedule or lesson plan. Be gentle; abused children respond positively to gentleness. Gentleness includes not forcing a child to be touched or hugged. This leads to patience. An abused child will need time to trust an adult. But bearing with a child until they trust you and even confide in you could change their life.

The passage goes on by encouraging us to use our gifts to build one another up in faith and to speak the truth in love, so that every part of the body is working in harmony, then ends with, "Be kind to one another, tenderhearted, forgiving one another, as God in Christ forgave you" (Ephesians 4:32). What a soothing balm it would be for a victim of childhood sexual abuse to be in this kind of relationship with their church family.

The unwillingness of the church or other Christians to talk about the issues surrounding sexual abuse piles on the shame, making a Christian victim feel like a second-class Christian. They suffer in silence because we just don't talk about such things in church. Well, the issues Christians who have been sexually abused face are real and they are unpleasant and uncomfortable to talk about. Ephesians 5:8–11 tells us, "For at one time you were darkness, but now you are light in the Lord. Walk as children of light (for the fruit of light is found in all that is good and right and true), and try to discern what is pleasing to the Lord. Take no part in the unfruitful works of darkness, but, instead, expose them." What could be more pleasing to the Lord than to rescue his children from darkness?

It is time for the church to look past the ugliness of abuse and help victims find freedom in Christ. Only the church—Christian brothers and sisters—can do that. The world can offer coping mechanisms, but true freedom in found only in Christ. We must overcome our squeamishness so that victims can find freedom from the hold these issues have on their lives. It is a lie of Satan that we must suffer in silence, and it can lead to all sorts of problems, from emotional issues to eating disorders to crippling shame to seeking acceptance outside of the church.

The years since my abuse have been filled with love, joy, and peace. Even though the memory of abuse is never far from me, and at times I still cry when I talk about it, the tears are not because of the memories. The tears are because I am overwhelmed by what God has done in my life. There is no greater joy than to serve God by serving his people, helping them through difficult circumstances, and pointing them to the love of their Savior. I am thankful for all I have suffered because of how God has used it in my life to help others. It was not without purpose.

And even if I never helped another person because of it, my suffering brought me to a place where all I had was Christ. Those were the times when I had the deepest intimacy with Jesus, when my faith and relationship with my Lord grew exponentially. For that I am eternally grateful.

About the Author

Childhood is far removed from me. The abuse I have written about ended almost forty years ago, although that doesn't seem possible. Some things about it I have forgotten. Others are as clear as the day they happened. The abuser was arrested in a separate case, and my abuse became public twenty-nine years ago. This book is the story I never wanted to write. I never wanted it to be a part of my life, and I certainly never wanted to share it publicly. God had other plans though, and I hope that my story is helpful to someone.

Many years have passed since the events described in this book. So who am I now? You may recall that even twenty-nine years ago, when people first found out about my history of abuse, they thought it couldn't be true because I was so "together." And that is true. I've had a wonderful, joy-filled life. It took a long time for me to find complete freedom from my past, but I got there. Praise God!

Doug and I have been married for over thirty-two years. He continues to be my rock when my life gets a little crazy. We've had a multitude of great times together and look forward to many more. The notion that marriage is hard has never been our reality. Marriage has come easy to us, probably because we both recognize that we're selfish people and try to put the other first in everything. He is the love of my life and is still tall, dark (although more salt than pepper these days), and handsome.

I am the mom of three boys—well, men now. All three are married, and I have the three best daughters-in-law a mom could ask for (and in my opinion, it was easier to raise boys and acquire the girls later). They have changed my title to Mom-Mom by giving us four grandchildren (so far), the little joys of my life.

Our oldest son went to college in California and stayed there. Let that be a lesson to all parents helping their children choose a college. Although he has chosen to live almost three thousand miles away from home, I don't hold it against him. San Diego is my happy place! We visit whenever possible to see our two granddaughters and their parents too, and soak up some sun and ocean breezes.

Our middle son serves as the Pastor of Youth and Family at our church. That's right, I am under his authority now. He and his wife have a three-year-old daughter and a newborn son. I hang out with these grandkids a few days each week. They brighten my days, make me laugh, and remind me that I am getting old.

My baby, who promised when he was four that would always be my little boy, is twenty-three and got married in January 2017. They don't have children yet, but they do have a puppy. Twins run in my daughter-in-law's family, so I am hopeful for multiple more grandchildren. (They love when I say that.) He has followed in his dad's footsteps and works in the operating room as a surgical scrub technician.

I have a group of friends called the Sisterchicks (see Robin Gunn Jones series of books—pretty sure she just followed us around and wrote it all down). We have crazy adventures together, laugh until we leak, and lean on each other in times of trial. I couldn't do life without them. But I will deny anything that appears in overseas police reports or tabloids.

For over thirty-five years, I have served as a volunteer in youth ministry and still love being involved in it. I keep telling people that my next book will be a funny one titled *Youth Ministry: The First Twenty-Five Years Are the Hardest*. After that, the kids really don't expect much from you. You don't have to play their games, and you shouldn't. You could break a hip. They're just happy that you show up, laugh at their jokes, and bake brownies. Everything else is gravy.

Teaching God's Word is my real joy, so I do it whenever I can. I do that through our Ladies Bible Study and speaking engagements. While there was little humor in this book, I am actually a very funny person, at least I think so. And I like to teach with a balance of seriousness and humor. Life can be so hard; it's good to laugh whenever you have the opportunity.

I also love to shop, especially for shoes. If all you can tell about me by my outward appearance is that I have great shoes, I'm okay with that. Sports is one of my loves, especially football, volleyball, and baseball. Yes, I do know every rule and everything that should have happened in every game. My children do not like watching games with me. That's fine because they are wrong about other things too. They think curling is a sport. I accept them as they are. A mother's love.

I used to love to exercise, run, play volleyball, rock climb, kayak, etc., but I have developed some physical issues in the past two years that are very limiting and may become the basis for another book. My advice: Take black box warnings on medications very seriously and ask your doctor if there is another medication without the side effects that they could substitute. But my issues have given me time to sit down and write, so all things certainly do work for good for those who love God.

My hobbies include quilting (hand quilting, none of that new-fangled machine quilting), writing, reading, cooking, traveling, playing Play-Doh (aka hanging with the grandkids), and raising puppies for The Seeing Eye, Inc. For sixteen years I had the best job in the world, as an Area Coordinator in Puppy Development at The Seeing Eye, Inc. I basically got to visit people and play with their puppies. Occasionally, I helped someone solve a behavior problem too. Puppy raising and child raising are very similar, except for with one you can use a crate. With the other one, you must learn to deal with it and pray they go back to sleep. That job also gave me a platform to hone my speaking skills, something I never thought I would need.

My life has been filled with special moments, belly laughs, peaks and valleys, and more belly laughs. It really was a normal, joy-filled life that from the outside was devoid of any hint of abuse. My prayer in writing this book is that someone will read it and find the freedom in Christ that I found so many years ago—and that they too would have their past hidden with Christ and live a truly abundant life.

I wish you God's richest blessings!

Lisa

Endnotes

1 "The Refiner's Touch," *Clarion Call*, accessed December 6, 2017, http://www.clarion-call.org/extras/malachi.htm.

2 Charles Haddon Spurgeon, *Devotional Classics of C. H. Spurgeon* (Mulberry, Indiana: Sovereign Grace Publishers, 2008), July 19 morning reading.

3 Alistair Begg, *Made for His Pleasure* (Chicago: Moody Press, 1996), 39.

4 William Eleazar Barton, *The Life of Clara Barton: Founder of the American Red Cross, Volume 2* (New York: Houghton Mifflin, 1922), 345.

5 Martin Rogers, "Arrest of Jerry Sandusky's son reopens old wounds," *USA Today*, February 13, 2017, accessed December 7, 2017, https://www.usatoday.com/story/sports/columnist/martin-rogers/2017/02/13/jerry-sandusky-son-jeffrey-child-sexual-abuse/97870072/.

6 John Piper, *The Pleasures of Being God: Meditations on God's Delight in Being God* (Sisters, Oregon: Multnomah, 2000), 244.

7 Christopher Love, *Grace: The Truth and Growth and Different Degrees Thereof* (London: 1810), 80.